Back in Time
Growing up in the Applegate

by
Evelyn Byrne Williams
with Janeen Sathre

Editors
Laura Ahearn, President, McKee Bridge Historical Society
Diana Coogle, Chair, *Applegater* Newsmagazine Board of Directors

ISBN 979-8-9866994-0-0

Applegater Newsmagazine
PO Box 14
Jacksonville, OR 97530

McKee Bridge Historical Society
8595 Upper Applegate Road
Jacksonville, OR 97530

Cover Photo. Palmer Creek enters the Applegate River at the historic Silva, McKee, and Byrne farms, c. 1970.

Photo Credits. Most of the photographs in this book are from the collections of Evelyn Byrne Williams and other McKee and Byrne family members. Exceptions are noted in the captions.

Published by N8tive Run Press, a subsidiary of N8tive Run Enterprises, 5007 Laurel Avenue, Grants Pass, OR 97527.

Acknowledgments

Thanks to Laura Ahearn for turning her meticulous eye for historical accuracy on this manuscript and for the initial organizing of the material.

Thanks to *Applegater* board members Jessica Bullard and Michael Schneider for retyping some of the "Back in Time" articles from the newspaper itself into digital format.

Thanks to Janeen Sathre for coordinating between her mother and the production crew.

Special thanks to Rachel Harris, Southern Oregon University intern with the *Applegater* in 2021, for the hours she spent helping us get the newspaper columns into book format.

Thanks to Lisa Baldwin, *Applegater* board member and owner of N8tive Run Press, for proofreading.

Thanks to Barbara Holiday for design and layout.

And, especially, thanks to Evelyn Byrne Williams for sharing these stories with us and for her patience with the publication process.

Table of Contents

Introduction

From its first or second year of publication (1994-95), the *Applegater*, then a bimonthly newsmagazine for the Applegate Valley of southern Oregon, included a column about Applegate history, called "Way Back When," written by Myrtle Krause or John and Marguerite Black. Evelyn Byrne Williams's first piece was probably in the March-April 2005 issue. (The records are incomplete, but we do know that her second piece was in the May-June 2005 issue.) She called her column "Back in Time" and for many years delighted readers with her reminiscences of growing up in the Applegate, supplemented with diaries from Applegate inhabitants "back in time," stories she had been told, research from other Applegate historians and writers, and wonderful old photographs. In her columns readers enjoyed hearing about old gas pumps in the area as much as about the time Evelyn's sister locked her in the rabbit hutch; about her parents' car trip to Victoria, British Columbia, from her father's diary, as much as about the Logtown Cemetery.

Readers were charmed. Was it really within a living person's lifetime that people rode mules and crossed the river on swinging bridges and did laundry by hand with a wringer washing machine? How different the Applegate is today!

The great-granddaughter of pioneers John and Maryum McKee, Evelyn was the perfect person to take us back in time in the Applegate. The McKees arrived in the Rogue Valley from Missouri in 1853, first farming land at the foot of Roxy Ann Peak, then moving to the mining town of Logtown, in the Applegate. The McKee name has been added to the history of the area, along with the Native American tribe names, Dakubetede, Takelma, and Shasta, and other pioneer names mentioned in this book.

But Evelyn wasn't writing a history book. She was simply writing down a memory about one episode or another from those days back in time. She didn't write her first column about her great-grandparents, the McKees; she reminisced instead about a dance at the Applegate Grange: "I recall the first time I went to the Applegate Grange Hall, probably at five years of age, with my parents, John and Pearl Byrne, for a dance." She continues to tell some history about the Applegate Grange, of which her Aunt Clara was a charter member, and to describe, in the beautiful language of nostalgia, her memories of good times there:

Memories abound for me whenever I pass the place where the Grange once stood. I can still hear the friendly voices, often with laughter, and the dance music. Grange meetings were somewhat boring for me then, but it is those kind faces I recall the most. My heart is filled with gratitude for having been with these wonderful people who were once the early settlers in the Applegate Valley.

Evelyn's last piece for her column was called "Learning to Sew" and was totally out of chronological order, since it was about her teen years. But "Back in Time" wasn't chronological; it wasn't meant to tell a coherent story. It was a series of reminiscences by someone with a sharp memory and a delightful storytelling style.

Now this book brings Evelyn's stories back to us. The editors, Laura Ahearn and Diana Coogle, have put these stories roughly in chronological order, but no attempt has been made to turn a series of columns into a history book. There are inevitable repetitions and inaccuracies. Even Evelyn's memory isn't infallible. Egregious errors have been corrected, for the historical record, but the editors have chosen to let each piece stand on its own, as it did in its original printing in the *Applegater*.

These short essays have special poignance for me, as I am Evelyn Byrne Williams's daughter. I live on the family land on Palmer Creek, across the road from my mother. I am a fifth-generation Applegater, and my mother's memories about my family and this land take me back in time in a personal way.

Now I invite you to open this book and take a trip "back in time."

Janeen Sathre
Palmer Creek, Applegate, Oregon

A Byrne Family Episode

Even before I was born, my parents and older siblings had lived in the Applegate Valley. Sadly, though, they had been forced to leave the area when their ranch on Squaw Creek (now mostly under the Applegate Lake) was lost because my parents could not pay off the bank loan taken out to buy some cattle. Unfortunately, by the time the cattle were ready to sell, the market was down, and they had no other way to cover the loan.

Amos and Lottie McKee, my maternal grandparents, lived across the Applegate River from the mouth of the Palmer Creek, where my parents and their three small children stayed while Dad looked for employment. This he found in Topsy, Oregon, not far from Klamath Falls, as a logger. Pearl (my mother), Morris (brother), and Aletha (sister) moved to the logging camp to be with John (father), leaving my sister Gladys with Grandpa and Grandma, as she had fallen asleep just before they were to leave. Grandma said she could stay until Mother and Dad came back in a couple of weeks to pick up more of their belongings. This proved to be a blessing.

After living in the logging camp only a few days, my mother, brother, and sister (Aletha) became very ill with a severe intestinal ailment. Dad was working out in the woods when someone came for him. He came back to find his three-year-old daughter dead and his wife and son so sick that he feared for their lives too. How they survived the long journey to Medford to receive medical treatment I cannot imagine, and then my poor father had to make funeral arrangements while still worried about his family.

The sad family returned once again to the Applegate and the grandparents' home, where everyone was thankful that Gladys had stayed. Dad went back to the logging camp to retrieve the family belongings and then once again went looking for work.

At the McKee Farm in 1920, l-r: Harry Howard, Amos McKee,
Gladys Byrne, Lottie and Clara McKee, and Pearl McKee Byrne holding Aletha.

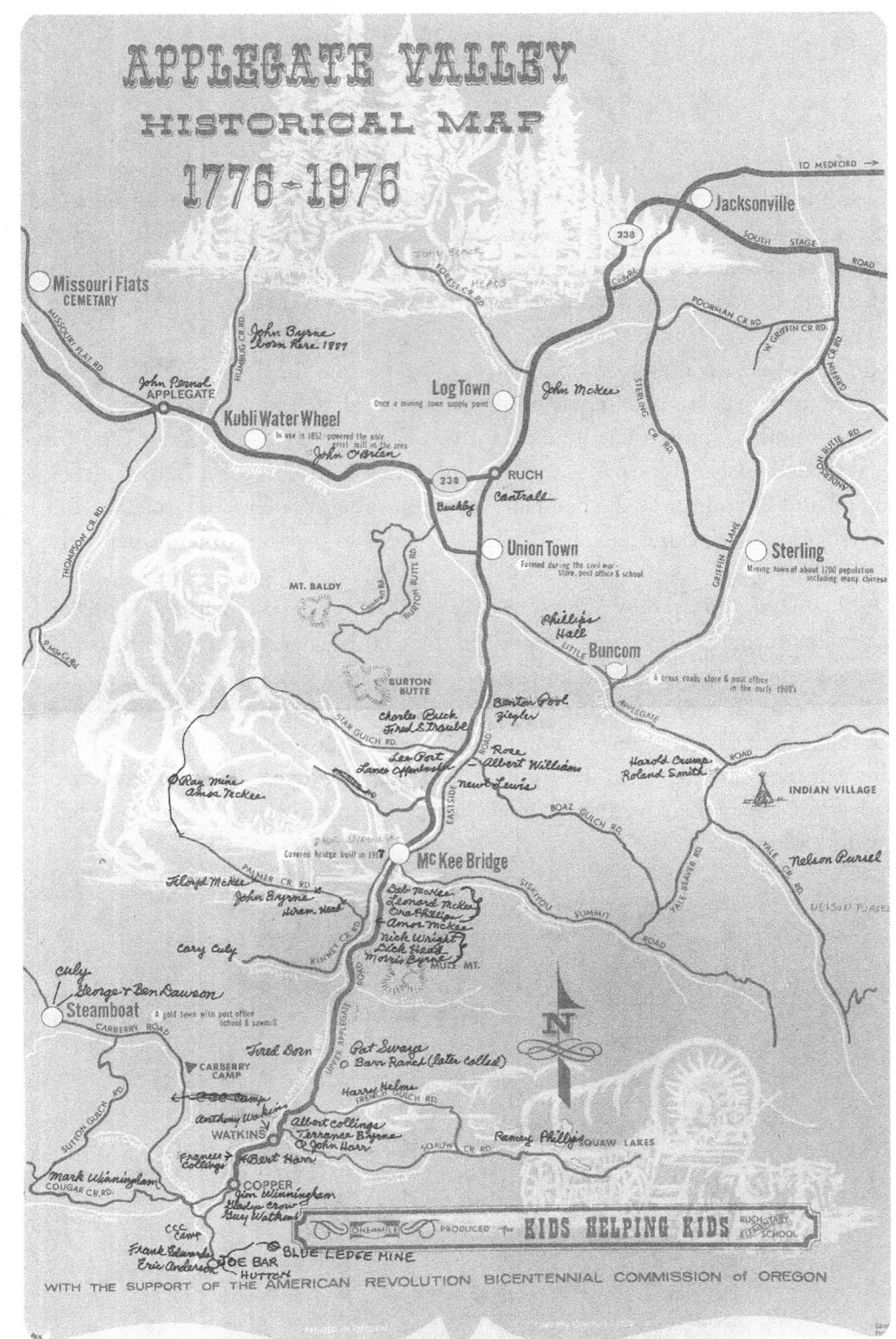

1976 Bicentennial map annotated by Evelyn.

Life in Medford

Dad found work at the mill of the Owen-Oregon Lumber Company, in Medford. My family once again left the upper reaches of the Applegate River Valley and the loving home of my grandparents (Amos and Lottie McKee). A house on North Central in Medford was available to rent, and since we had little to move, it quickly became a home.

I was born there three years later, in 1926. I don't remember much of this house, as it was not too long after my birth that we moved to a house on West Sixth Street. Morris and Gladys went to Washington School, where the Jackson County Courthouse is now. Our neighbors on Sixth Street were the Perls, who owned and operated the Perl Funeral Home. I remember my parents saying they were good neighbors, and they became good friends of the family.

I remember one incident, which was talked about in my family many times. The Perls kept rabbits in a large hutch in their backyard, and I enjoyed petting them. One day my mother was very busy, so she told my sister, Gladys, who was about 10, to take care of me for a while. We went over to look at the rabbits. While we were there, some of Gladys's friends came by, wanting her to play with them. Not wanting me to be running around alone, she put me in the hutch and locked the door. I remember being very content there. Gladys returned home having forgotten about me, to find mother frantic as to where I might be. They raced over to the hutch, finding me safe and sound, having a nap. Needless to say, Gladys never caged me again.

Then there was the time my grandpa came to town in his Model T Ford coupe. He hardly knew how to drive, so Grandma had stayed home, where she felt much safer. He stopped to see us and before leaving asked me if I would like to go home with him after he did his shopping. Of course, I did, so I went to collect the clothes I thought I needed and my doll. Then I went outside to await his return. I waited and waited and waited. Grandpa never came back that day. I learned that he had a teasing nature, and after that day I was wary of what he might be teasing me about.

The doll I was going to take with me that day was an expensive one given to me by someone other than my mother or father, but who that person was is lost in time. I loved that doll dearly and played with it often. One day a little girl stopped by to play with me on our front porch. We played house, using the porch bench as a bed for the doll. After we were done, I failed to take my doll inside the house, and the next morning it was gone. I cried and cried. As no one could have seen it from the sidewalk, I have often wondered if that little girl took my doll.

My mother and father planted a large garden at the back of the house where an old barn had been. This ground was very fertile, and the garden produced more than we could use. Morris found a set of cart wheels at the county dump and built a wooden bed on them. This became his wagon to take the extra vegetables around the neighborhood to sell. Mother rented the unused upstairs rooms for added income, and our family began to prosper.

When I was three years old, Gladys took me to my first movie show at the Holly Theatre. What a treat that was! All I remember was a man trying to get his very heavy-set wife into a small car. He tried all kinds of ways of doing it, all of which were very funny. When he finally did get her in, they drove away with her side of the car leaning at a 45-degree angle. Regretfully, it was the last movie I was to see until 1939, when I saw *Gone with the Wind* at the same Holly Theatre.

Noted in Pearl Byrne's handwriting: "Evelyn and her wardrobe ready to go to Grandma's, about three years old, 408 West 6th Street."

Summer of '29

By 1929 my parents were somewhat prospering after having left the Applegate and moved to Medford, where Dad found employment at the Owen-Oregon sawmill. They were renting a two-story house at 408 West Sixth Street next to the Perl Funeral home. The Perls and my folks became good friends, and I often took the liberty of playing on their front steps or visiting their rabbits that they kept in a hutch in the backyard.

Mother was making some money by renting the rooms upstairs in our house. I sometimes got permission to visit a nice couple living up there, who would make me bread-and-honey sandwiches. I was not to play on the stairs, though I found it difficult not to do this. However, the closet underneath the stairway became a terrifying place that I had to stay in sometimes when being naughty. The threat of being there made me an almost model child.

My brother, Morris, and sister, Gladys, attended the Washington School, where the Jackson County Courthouse is located now. It was close enough to our home for my sister to sometimes take me there after school to play on the slide and swings. Most of all, I wanted to be able to roller skate as my sister was doing when she took me there, but my feet were too small for skates to be screwed onto my shoes. Those old skates would probably be a collector's item now.

One day a city crew was making sidewalks by our house. When they left, Morris took the liberty to write his name in the fresh cement on the corner of Sixth and Ivy Streets. Maybe it is still there. Of course, the old house is long gone, and the Evelyn apartments are there in its place. The name is just a coincidence.

I remember the long hot summer in 1929, when my mother convinced my dad to take us on a weekend trip to the coast. None of us had ever seen the ocean, and the thought of getting out of the heat for a while was so inviting. We had a Chevrolet touring car, maybe a 1919 model, with a canvas top.

It was a long ride to Crescent City, California, especially in those days. The dirt roads were bumpy and dusty, and riding in the back seat and enduring all of the wind and particles in the air while getting car sick definitely put a damper on the first part of my trip. However, seeing the beautiful big redwood trees was wonderful. Mother took a picture of us by our car, but the mystery is why she didn't take any pictures of the giant trees.

Getting a flat tire was one of the worst parts of traveling in those days. My poor dad had to stop and patch an inner tube several times before reaching our destination in the late evening, when we would rent a small cabin for the night. I recall there being about four or five of these cabins down by the beach. Gladys had disappeared from us while our car was being unloaded. She had always been inquisitive, and by the time my mother found her, she was getting acquainted with some people in another cabin.

Our cabin was not at all cheerful, but we were so glad to get out of the cold wind. Mother made our beds, but she realized she had not brought enough bedding to keep us warm. No one was able to sleep, so when early morning came, we hurriedly piled back into the car and left. I do not remember seeing the ocean as I was too miserable to remember anything but the cold.

On the way home, we sort of welcomed the intense heat, but poor Dad kept having to fix flat tires. I'm sure he was not having a good time with this trip. About four blocks from home, he didn't even stop to fix another flat; we just kept on going, and Gladys was so embarrassed that someone would see us that Dad let her out of the car to walk the rest of the way home.

Soon after this trip the Great Depression came, and we moved back to the Applegate in the summer of 1930. I did not return to see the ocean until 1948. The beautiful Oregon Coast became one of my favorite places to go, and the traveling was so much better than on that first trip back in time.

John, Evelyn, and Gladys Byrne.

Gladys and Evelyn Byrne in their front yard.

Return to Family Roots at Palmer Creek

When the Great Depression hit in 1929, Dad lost his job. He immediately went to draw his money out of the local bank and felt fortunate to receive a part of his money, $200, before foreclosure closed the doors of the bank for good.

Dad joined other men on the streets of Medford asking for any kind of work. One day he happened to meet a friend from Applegate, Lee Port, a US Forest Service ranger from Star Ranger Station. When Lee found out how desperate my dad was for a job, he said he could use him to clean some mountain trails. It was a miracle for us. Even though the job was only during the summer months, my folks wanted to return to the Applegate, and now they could.

In 1930 we moved into a rented house, where I remember being able to see the covered McKee Bridge from our front yard. The road, dirt all the way from Ruch, was close to our house, but few cars came by to raise the dust. Other things were also different from living in Medford. There was no electricity, and the neighborhood sounds were not the same.

I remember waking up one night to the haunting sound of howling coyotes, which I had never heard before. They sounded as if they were right outside my bedroom window. I screamed and ran, jumping into bed with my parents. They had a very difficult time getting me to go into my room at bedtime after that. This changed after we moved to a miner's cabin on the west side of the Applegate River near the mouth of Palmer Creek, where I could hear the enchanting sound of running water instead of coyotes. [See "Remembering an Old Log Cabin," page 118.]

We did not live in the miner's cabin very long before moving into our unfinished three-bedroom house, built on land that my grandparents owned. A carpenter friend was hired to erect it, and we moved in when the roof, outside siding, windows, and doors were finished. Mother tacked some blankets and quilts on the exposed studded walls for privacy. Since it was still winter, the kitchen with the cook stove was the only warm place in the house. That is where we would stay until bedtime and then take heated rocks wrapped in newspaper to bed to keep our feet warm.

The next big change for me was school. My brother, Morris, left to stay with mother's sister and her husband, Clara and Jack O'Brien, who lived down lower Applegate. From there he could ride the bus to the Jacksonville High School. My sister, Gladys, walked to the Beaver Creek School, about a mile north of us on the east side of the river. When I started school, I, too, took this walk across the river on a wire fence footbridge. The bridge was quite high off the river and hung from cables attached to large trees on each side of the river. The west side of the river was lower than the east, so there was a narrow wooden up-ramp on our side of the bridge. I remember Dad having to scoop the snow off as best he could after a winter storm, and we would put wool socks or large pieces of a gunnysack over our galoshes to help keep us from sliding on the wooden walkway of the bridge.

Every winter brought at least three to twelve inches of snow, so by the time we reached the school, we were wet and cold up to our knees. Once on the east side of the river, we would follow our teacher's footprints coming from my grandparents' house, where most of the teachers boarded, to the school. She would leave early enough to have the old potbelly stove heated up so the children could warm up and dry out before class started. The stove had a high shield around it that made a good place to hang our wet stockings. Talk about one smelly room with steamy windows!

Byrne bridge near the author's home on Palmer Creek, 1933. L-R: Maud Byrne Watson, Mamie Foley, Bernard Watson, Florence McKee, Gladys Byrne, and Patrick Foley.

Workday at Beaver Creek School

When I look at the wonderful old photographs that I have collected over the years, I find myself reminiscing about the people and places captured in those pictures. One such photo transports me back to one of my favorite places, the Beaver Creek School, and memories of the friends and family gathered there.

This 1930 photo from Lee Port, Jr, was taken in back of the newer Beaver Creek School just before school started in September. I think everyone brought a lunch, or it could have been a potluck. My father, John Byrne, is there along with cousins, uncles, and my sister, Gladys, who is standing in the middle of the picture.

As you can see, the workday was well attended for that small school. The women swept and mopped the floors, cleaned windows inside and out, cleaned the desks, and checked underneath the seats for any hidden chewing gum. Some students were privileged to have that luxury (gum) while others made do with "pitch gum" found on pine trees. Still, both could be found stuck to the furniture and required some elbow grease to remove.

When the school building was spick-and-span, the cleaning chores moved to the outside privies. The boys' was behind the woodshed to the far left, and the girls' was at the far right, behind a large pine tree. A broom with a bucket of soapy water took care of the seats, and then someone held a sack of lime over the hole and dropped in about one quarter of its contents for sanitation. I think we used old catalogs instead of toilet paper. It was so much cheaper, and kids were used to the catalog bit.

The men either cut wood there or brought some for the old potbelly heating stove. It took a lot to keep the school warm during the winter because there was no insulation in the building. The woodshed is at the right of the photo, and I remember it being filled with wood. The children were not allowed to play in there, but the older boys could carry wood in for the stove. They seemed to like that task, even when the snow was a foot or two deep, as it often was. I remember how the teacher would let us sit near the stove during the winter when we got too cold for comfort at our desks.

One of the other things I remember is the small room inside the back door on the south side of the building where there was a coat closet for the boys and drinking water was piped in from a nearby spring to a faucet and sink. That was such a luxury for those who did not have running water in their homes.

It was sad when, after 47 years, there were not enough students for the school to continue operating. It closed in 1945. A few students left to attend Uniontown School. And then some consolidation with Ruch took place in the summer of 1946.

Front row, left to right: My dad, John Byrne; my cousin Virgil O'Brien (visiting from Pinole, CA); Floyd Rippey; Albert Andersen (boy); Cary Culy; and Edward Finley.
Second row: Wesley Ritchey (?); my uncle Floyd McKee; unknown; my aunt Eva McKee, with son, Richard; my sister, Gladys Byrne (who passed away in 2015 at age 97); Lester Andersen.
Back row: Unknown, unknown, unknown, unknown, Mamie Winningham.
Behind fence: Unknown, Maude Pool, George Peck, unknown, Louis Straube.

First year at Beaver Creek School

My first day in a one-room schoolhouse, in 1932, was so exciting it is more memorable than any other school day. I hardly slept the night before, just anticipating being there in a new dress that my mother had made, wearing my brand-new shoes and carrying a colorful lidded lunch pail.

To help my shyness at that time, I was so glad to have my sister, Gladys, along with me, even though she was much older, in the eighth grade. Also, my first cousin, Doug McKee, and my second cousin, Marcene McKee, would be joining me in the first grade.

I already knew the wonderful teacher, Miss Jeannette Gore, because she boarded at my grandparents' home. She was so very well liked and became a close friend of our family. Thus, I headed off on the mile-long walk to school with great anticipation of all the fun I would have on my first day at Beaver Creek School, often called McKee School.

Miss Gore greeted everyone and assigned seats. There was a primary table about three feet by six feet and maybe 20 inches high with six small chairs. (In later years I was given one of these chairs that my children and others enjoyed using.)

We had a first-grade reader and workbooks with about fifty pages, in which we copied the alphabet, made words, and wrote numbers. To me, the best part of the book was coloring the pictures. Sometimes we were told what colors to use, and other times we could create some of our own colorings. Miss Gore made a weekly inspection of our assignments, and we usually got As.

Recess was the best, but the playground did lack for equipment, except for a large slide, which I did not play on due to my fear of heights. Also, the older boys would wipe it with wax paper, always in good supply from our sandwich wrappers, which made for an extremely fast ride. "Anti-Over" was a favorite game with the older boys. This game consisted of two teams, one on each side of the school, throwing the ball back and forth over the roof. If you caught the ball, you got to throw it back over. The only other rule was to not break a window in the school building. To the best of my knowledge all windows remained unbroken.

And, of course, where would we be without the game of baseball? Our school lacked enough older students for a full team, so some of us younger children were reluctantly asked to fill in. One year we were taken to the Uniontown School to play a game, and I was scared to death that a ball would come my way! I don't recall who won, but I do remember the teacher at Uniontown was Miss Inlow, and ours was Mrs. Bertha Haskins. Priorities!

At Thanksgiving time, Miss Gore must have contacted our mothers about making some costumes in which to celebrate the season. We were dressed as Indians and pilgrims. I remember the scratchy gunnysack clothing we wore as the Indians, but I was very proud of the hand-painted designs and the turkey feather on our headbands. It is amazing to still have a couple of pictures of us in our costumes. It seemed as though that first year of school went faster than any other, and then I was looking forward to summer vacation.

On that last day of school, I was bragging to Marcene that my birthday was June 22 and that after lunch on that day I was going to have a big birthday party with a delicious birthday cake for all to enjoy.

Well, much to my regret, she remembered that date, and her mother brought her to our house for the celebration. I was shocked and so embarrassed, and my mother was totally flabbergasted. The truth was that no party had been planned, not even a cake baked because the wood cookstove made the house too hot in June. Lois, Marcene's mother, and my mother actually had a nice visit, but I never really got over that embarrassment!

Beaver Creek School.

Costumed students. Front row: Albert Andersen, Trueman "Bud" Lewis Jr., Carmoletta Lewis, unknown, Rosella Offenbacher, Clara Faye McKee, Evelyn Byrne. Back row: Gladys Byrne, Frances Port, Vonetta Rupretch, Lester Andersen, George Taylor (?), Victor Valdemar Andersen.

Beaver Creek School students who started the year 1934-1935. The girls, left to right, are Rosella Offenbacher, Clara Faye McKee, Evelyn Byrne. The boys, left to right, are Douglas McKee, Orden Phillips, Walter Offenbacher, Dean Phillips.

Beaver Creek School and students in the early 1920s. Back row: William Dietrick, Thelma Childers, Evelyn Childers, Lydia Lewis, Helen Culy, Dorothy McKee. Middle row: Omar Culy, Clara Faye McKee. Front row: Emmett Phillips, Ora Phillips, Earl Stephenson, Louis Culy.

A Special Grade-School Friend

When I started grade school at Beaver Creek School, my cousin Douglas McKee and a distant cousin of ours, Marcene McKee, were the only first-graders. Marcene and her family moved to Jacksonville before I was in second grade, and when Walter Offenbacher started school, he and Douglas got along right well. I missed having a girlfriend in my class. When the boys started bringing toy trucks to school and making roadways on the school's hillside, I felt very left out. It looked to be so much fun.

My mother surprised me one day with a little toy pick-up she had bought when she was shopping in Medford. It was bright red with white wheels. (It is the only toy I remember her buying.) I was so happy to take it to school and show everyone, but I chose to make my own roads on the hillside because I figured the boys didn't want me in their territory. I don't remember any other girls joining me.

Elsie Dietrick was the name of my special friend, and the toy car bit was over by the time she joined us in the fourth grade. Her family came here in 1934, during the Depression, and moved nearby, into a small log cabin, on the first mining claim up Palmer Creek. She had two brothers, Loren, older than she, and Harry Jr., the youngest. This was the first family with children during that time to live on Palmer Creek. There were quite a few other miners up there, but I only remember two who had wives; the rest were bachelors.

It is interesting how well Elsie and I got along. We never had any disagreement as most children do sometimes. We liked doing the same things, and our teacher would let us study together away from the other students if we had finished our homework. We could go into the library room or the girls' coat room, our favorite place, where we would go into a small closet and sit on the top shelf to look out the small, high window.

It didn't take long for Elsie's family to get acquainted with mine. Her parents, Harry and Hilda, liked to play a card game called Pedro with my folks. The family would walk down some evenings before dark to have some enjoyable card games. The adults played in the living room with the door closed, and we kids played cards and other games at the kitchen table. We were cautioned to not "rough house" because kerosene lamps had to be protected, as well as the rest of the kitchen. We had so much fun, and the time seemed to go too fast before they had to leave for home.

Often times, Elsie was asked to stay all night with me, especially on a Friday, after school. One Friday is quite memorable! I decided we needed a special treat after the mile walk home from school. Hungry for candy, we started making our own. We blended some powdered sugar and butter together with some red food coloring to get a luscious pink candy. Even though it was before the evening meal, we ate all we could hold. Sometime in the middle of the night, I became very ill and was unable to keep from throwing up over the side of the bed. Of course, this woke Elsie up, and I was so embarrassed to find Elsie's shoes the target of my distress. My mother had to clean everything up, so no one got much sleep that night. To this day I cannot stand the sight of any kind of pink candy or frosting.

I don't know how Elsie was able to forgive me or if her shoes were ever the same. However, she did invite me to stay all night with her, which pleased me. I so enjoyed being in the one-room log cabin, as it was the first time I had ever been inside one. It seemed so cozy with that nice family. I prayed that I would not eat something to cause another nighttime episode. Of course, it was difficult for Elsie and me to go to sleep and not disturb her family with our giggles. I don't recall how all the beds were arranged in such a small area. In those times one had to make do.

My uncle, Ernest McKee, got word to us that his family was moving from Klamath Falls to Cottage Grove, Oregon. They had a player piano they did not want to take with them, and he said my folks could have it for $50.00. During the Depression, that was a lot of money, but my dad thought it would be especially nice for my sister and me to learn to play. I don't know how he was able to get that much money, but since he was known as "honest John," I am sure he didn't steal it. Anyway, Dad contacted Mr. Dietrick, who had a fairly new pick-up, and they went to Klamath Falls for that wonderful piano. It had some piano rolls with it, so our house was constantly being filled with the roller music or our own terrible playing. *[Note from Janeen Sathre: Mom still has this piano and the rolls, which I remember playing as I was growing up.]*

It didn't take long for our closest neighbor, miner Bill Oakes, to hear about our musical addition. He was English, and we thought his name was Mr. Bloats when he first introduced himself. It took some time before we found out it wasn't Bloats. He had built a cabin at the far end of our field, which belonged to my grandfather, Amos McKee, who let the miners build on his properties in return for a percentage of gold they might find and also to help him during haying season. One day he came to see our piano and sat down and started to play. To our amazement he played classical and other songs we knew. How I wish we had asked him about his background, as it was obvious that he had some formal training. In those days it wasn't proper to pry.

Elsie was here for three more years, finishing the seventh grade at Beaver Creek School. The family moved to Ruch, probably for her older brother to ride the bus into Jacksonville for high school. They lived in the old dance hall that Cap Ruch had built in 1900. Elsie finished the eighth grade there at Ruch and graduated from Jacksonville High, while I graduated from Medford High. Her folks eventually moved to Dunsmuir, California, and I communicated with Elsie less and less. We both married and were kept busy with household duties and raising our children. However, we never forgot each other.

When Elsie was living in Eugene, Oregon, and her mother, Hilda, was living in Shady Cove, Oregon, they came to see me. It was a wonderful surprise which brought back such wonderful memories. At Christmas time, we share our love for each other and news about what happened during the past year. Sometimes there is much happiness and sometimes much sorrow to write in our letters, but I have always felt so fortunate in having this classmate friend for so many years.

1933-34 School Picture, left to right:
Front Row: Orden Phillips, Harry Dietrick, Dean Phillips.
Middle Row: Douglas McKee, Walter Offenbacher, Elsie Dietrick, Evelyn Byrne.
Back Row: Clara Faye McKee, Lorne Dietrick, Rosella Offenbacher.

Independence Day in the Applegate

Celebrating the Fourth of July each year, we have a chance to reflect on how fortunate we are to have our independence. It was not easy for our forefathers to achieve a democracy and lead the way for us to become a great nation. There have been many ups and downs, but our freedoms are still worth honoring at least every Fourth of July.

I remember being awakened in the early morning of many a July Fourth with sounds of guns being fired up and down the Applegate. The guns of my grandfather and uncle on nearby farms were the loudest, almost like cannons. It was the beginning of a wonderful holiday for picnicking along a mountain stream with family and friends. Mother and my maternal grandmother would have fixed fried chicken, potato salad, cakes, and pies. Sometimes we had watermelons that were placed in the cold stream for a treat later in the afternoon. Someone always gave small firecrackers to us children. These were soon gone, but we always found other things to keep us busy until the end of the day. A dance somewhere that night was the grand finale, always seeming to end much too soon.

Before my time, many Fourth of July celebrations on the Applegate were big-time events, when whole neighborhoods would get together for a picnic. We would play all kinds of games. There would be horse races, speeches, and, best of all, baseball. Another celebration on May 5, 1901, at the John Buckley ranch on Hamilton Road, was about the most fashionable I have seen in a photo. Seated on the ground are at least 23 women in their best attire and wearing stylish hats. There is one man in the back row. Was he posing there as a joke or was he staying near his lady friend?

Universal Studios used this photograph in 1974 when they made *The Great Northfield Minnesota Raid* in Jacksonville. They copied the dress styles in this photo for their actors.

I've also seen a photo of around 26 men watching a baseball game with John Buckley as the catcher and James Buckley the batter. Universal Studios also filmed a baseball game in that same Buckley field for the movie!

I love the picture of the ball-throwing booth, star-spangled and all. This must have been a gentleman's sport, as there are no ladies present. The tallest man at the far right is Floyd McKee, and his uncle, "Deb" McKee, is standing next to him, with the dapper hat.

Of course, the bigger and grander July Fourth parties in towns and cities drew more crowds and attention with their parades and colorful nighttime fireworks displays. That is something most country folks were unable to attend, but it makes no difference how one celebrated our country's historic Independence Day. It was patriotism to the fullest extent, and it seemed as though it was a little more interesting back in time.

May 5, 1901. Front row, left to right: Bryant Hamilton (small boy), Ada Cameron Pool, Rose Buckley and Hazel Hamilton (young girl). Second row, left to right: Dora Bostwick Cameron, Emma Ulrich, ? (unidentified), Carrie Offenbacher, Molly Ray, ? (unidentified) and my aunt Stella Byrne. Mrs. Bauten is in the front seat of the buggy and Minnie (last name?) in the back seat.

Ball-throwing booth, July 4, 1914. Floyd McKee is the tall man on the right; Deb McKee is on his right. Leslie Moses stands in front of them. His brother, Roland, is in front of the table. Clarence Buck is on the left in the round white hat. Bert McKee is in suspenders and mustache.

Dad's Scary Hospital Experience

When I was about eight years old my dad was in bed for several days with a bad cold or the flu. Our family physician, Doctor Heckman, no longer made house calls as he did when my older brother and two sisters were born in 1916, 1918, and 1920. He would stay overnight and perhaps enjoy his favorite pastime, fishing the Squaw Creek or Applegate River, before returning home the next day.

This time Mother had to take Dad to Medford, where Doctor Heckman promptly sent him to Sacred Heart Hospital. Poor Mother returned home late that afternoon, very worried, and said for me to hurry and feed our chickens and gather eggs while she milked the cow. My brother and sister were not there to help, since they were living with my Aunt Clara in lower Applegate so they could ride the school bus to Jacksonville High School.

After our chores, Mother and I crossed the Applegate River on a footbridge and walked the quarter mile upriver to the McKee (my maternal grandparents') home, where we could make a phone call to find out about Dad. It turned out he had a serious ear infection requiring mastoid surgery. I was so frightened! I thought any surgery in those days could be fatal and had heard so many stories I thought my dad might die.

Mother assured me that Dad would be all right but told me that she and Grandma were taking Grandpa's car to the hospital and might not return until the next morning, so I would have to stay with Grandpa. I liked Grandpa, but I was very upset to be left behind.

The next day Mother said I could go with her to see Dad. It was a cold day, so we had to bundle up, especially since our old car was "open air," with no top. It had only a front seat with a wooden bed built on the back for hauling things like firewood and sacks of chicken feed.

I thought we should have taken Grandpa's car, a Durant sedan that Uncle Ernest (mother's oldest brother), a car salesman, had helped get for Grandpa. I first rode in it after my uncle moved his family to Klamath Falls and Grandma wanted to visit them, so Mother drove me, Grandma, and my sister, Gladys, to my uncle's for an overnight stay. I wanted another ride in that car and kept begging Mother to borrow it, but she refused.

So I pouted for most of the drive to Medford in our old car. When Mother had to stop at a stop sign, she found out that our car brakes were barely working. My pouting then turned into real fright. Mother drove in low gear all the way up the hill to the hospital. I wonder what was going through her mind about all the debt—the doctor, the hospital (no insurance in those days), and an old car in need of repair.

At the hospital we entered a large room, a ward, filled with male patients. Dad was propped up in bed in the middle of the room and very glad to see us. A nurse came in and angrily told my dad that he was not to move his bed. She ignored Mother and me, keeping up her tirade at Dad as she shoved the bed back against the wall.

When the nurse left, Mother asked Dad what in the world was going on. He explained that he was very cold, so had moved his bed away from the cold brick wall and a window. My dad was of a gentle nature and avoided trouble. He had probably never been "chewed out" so much. I could not believe seeing my mother so calm about the incident and Dad, still in some pain, beginning to see some humor in it. Dad was still cold, though, so mother found a kind nurse to help get Dad warmed up. It took a long time before Dad thawed out and became more comfortable. When he got drowsy, we kissed him good-bye and quietly left.

Mother went slowly down the hill through Medford, always in low gear. I kept telling her she should have taken Grandpa's car.

Pearl and John Byrne, aka Mother and Dad, late 1917.

The Honey Robbers

Each year in September my father would say, "It is time to get the bait out for the honeybees." Even though the family felt bad about robbing the poor bees of their winter supply of honey, the act was sanctioned as a necessity for our food supply.

The Applegate had many oak trees that were nearly or completely dead with a hollow inside for the bees to store their honey. By late fall, the nests were filled with an abundance of delicious honey, and we could hardly wait to enjoy it. Many of our neighbors also hunted bee trees. We followed a code of ethics to not infringe on a tree with a name marked on it. Often we would find a marked tree after many hours or days of hunting, and we would have to begin again.

First, we chose a warm bare hillside. Then my father would place the bait— honey or sweet anise, which he felt worked better than sugar water—in a small pan, and we waited for the bees. Sometimes it would take an hour or more before a bee would come and take its fill. The bee, now weighted down, would fly very slowly, making it easier to track its destination. We could estimate how far away the nest might be by waiting for the returning bee with its comrades. The bait was moved from time to time to get closer to the nest.

When we found the tree at last, we had to decide whether we had enough time to proceed with the robbery or if we should leave our name on the tree and harvest another day. If there was time to get the honey, my father conducted a survey to see how to fell the tree without damaging the honey. Those working near the hive needed proper clothing, such as a heavy coat and trousers, gloves, and a see-through covering over a hat to drape down over the shoulders. Next, they placed a smoking fire of sulfur in a small can at the base of the tree or in an opening in the lower part of the tree, forcing the bees to the top of the nest. Although most of the bees would die from the sulfur, sometimes an angry swarm would come out, attacking anything that moved. When things calmed down, the tree was cut.

Just to see the honey was amazing—structures of wax in hexagonal cells, row upon row, sometimes several feet long and a foot or so wide. Usually the honey and comb were light golden in color, but occasionally they would be very dark and not palatable, being several years old. Also, even though the honey looked good, it might have had an undesirable taste due to the type of nectar gathered by the bees. Honey tasted different in the higher elevations, with a stronger, more flavorful taste. Most of the honey we had was rather mild, probably because of the alfalfa fields.

After the bee tree was cut, the honey was carefully taken out, and any part with bee bread or bee larva was thrown away. We put the slabs of good honeycomb in large containers with lids. By the time we returned home, there would be at least a quart of liquid honey in the bottom. My mother would put this into jars to be used for cooking or pouring over pancakes. The honey left in the comb would be spread on bread or biscuits along with our country butter or thick cream. Often times the honey would go to sugar, which I thought was the best because it tasted like candy.

One time my brother, Morris, was stung on both sides of his face while cutting down a bee tree. After several hours the swelling changed his thin face to a fat one. Being unrecognizable, he decided to have some fun with his misery. He went to our grandmother's house and knocked on her door. When she opened it, he pretended to be a salesman of some sort, and she responded by inviting him in. Our grandmother thoroughly enjoyed company, and the Watkins or Fuller Brush salesmen were always welcomed. My brother kept going on and on about some product until he could no longer contain his deception or laughter. She still did not recognize him, thinking he was acting strange. "Grandma, it's me!" he exclaimed. "I've gotten stung by some honeybees and have brought you some of their honey."

She realized now who he was, and both had much laughter over the incident, which was retold many times in our family.

As some of the pictures show, honey was not the only food harvested in the fall to fill the larders for the winter months.

Heading home with honey cans filled with bounty for the winter.

After we cut down the bee tree, we carefully took out the honey and threw away any part with bee bread or bee larva.

Filling the larder with venison for the long winter ahead.

Adding a little bear meat to vary the winter diet.

School Days in the 1930s

One winter the river froze completely over with about five inches of ice. It must have been during the Christmas holidays because my brother, Morris, was home from high school. The snow sled he had made for sliding down the hills was now used to pull me up and down the river on the ice, much to my delight.

We were also able to take a shortcut to visit our grandparents on the other side of the river without having to go over the swinging bridge farther down river. I do not remember how long the river stayed frozen, but it was long enough that school was back in session. Several schoolmates who did not live next to the river wanted to play on the ice, even over a deep part known as the swimming hole in the bend of the river. The ice had melted some, so I told them they might fall through, but they laughed and called me "chicken," which upset me. They were having so much fun on that ice without any trouble that I decided to venture forth on the part close to the bank. Fortunately for us no one fell through.

My Beaver Creek School days were some of the happiest times of my life, even though, from the first grade until I reached the age of fifteen, I had the flu every winter. The flu was so severe I would miss at least a month of school each year. It was a real challenge trying to catch up with my studies. However, being in a one-room school had its advantages, as I learned many things from the grades ahead of me. I went through all eight grades with only four in my class; the total attendance was about fourteen children.

When I was in the fourth grade the teacher thought we should have a hot lunch in the wintertime. She organized a schedule for us to take turns fixing the hot meals. Our mothers were to supply the food, usually brought from home in a kettle, which could be put on the kerosene stove the teacher had set up on a table in the boys' cloakroom. I don't know how some of the children, who lived far away, managed to carry the food to school—like the Offenbachers, a sister and brother, who usually rode a horse, since they lived at least five miles away, near the Star Ranger Station—but they did.

At one time we had a removable stage in our small school building. Our teacher, Mrs. Haskins, had her carpenter husband build it. Our mothers made draw curtains from gray outing flannel. These curtains were supported on a tight wire across the front of the stage. The first stage production was a very exciting event for us, and the whole neighborhood was involved in the venture.

A play was written, a cast chosen, and evening rehearsals scheduled for the adults. We children had our own play and a harmonica band, which practiced right after school. We were sent home with a pattern for our mothers to make short blue capes and pillbox hats for the band performance. All of this was so exciting for us children, who had never been involved in anything like this before, that it was very hard waiting for the opening night.

I think I was to recite a poem. I know my voice quivered and became almost a whisper when I stood alone on the stage. When all my classmates had finished their parts, the adults began their play. One of our mothers, who had a leading part, went on stage and started crying. Everyone began clapping for her gifted performance until they found out she was overcome with stage fright and was not acting. It was all very exciting.

Another time, the teacher invited everyone to the school for an evening performance of a trapeze act. The man and woman trapeze artists had secured their swings to the ceiling. The room was filled to capacity, and everyone was in awe, since a live act of this type was a first for most of us. People talked about that for a long time.

Winter at the Byrne home on the Applegate River.

Schoolgirls, left to right: (front row) Evelyn Byrne, Grace Moore, Rosella Offenbacher, Carmoletta Lewis, Clara Faye McKee, Marcene McKee; (back row) Shirley Anne Crosby, Audrey Fletcher, Frances Port, Vonetta Rupretch, Gladys Byrne, Shirley Lewis.

Schoolboys, left to right: Douglas McKee, Albert Andersen, George Taylor, Robert Fletcher, Lester Andersen, Victor Andersen, Trueman Lewis Jr.

APPLEGATE RIVER IS FROZEN OVER

APPLEGATE, Dec. 17.—(Special)— Applegate people report report much damage by the freezing weather. The water pipes were frozen in houses and milk houses and much fruit and vegetables lost from freezing when the thermometer dropped near zero or below in some places. Several seem to be enjoying it, however, with the river and creeks frozen over, making good skating. Old timers here say this is the first time the river has been frozen over for about 40 years. Reports coming from Squaw lake are that it is covered with ice.

Applegate River freezes. Medford Mail Tribune, *December 18, 1932.*

The Love of Dancing

I grew up in a family who loved to dance. That actually began in 1853, with my great-grandfather, John McKee. He was the blacksmith at the gold-mining town of Logtown, on Forest and Poormans creeks, between Jacksonville and Ruch. Many Saturday night dances were in his family's home, where he also taught dancing. Of course, his children and their children on down followed that tradition.

I remember when a fiddle player, maybe the only musician, would be at some home, playing his heart out for a room full of dancers. I was about four years old when I first experienced such an event. It was in some neighbor's home in our Upper Applegate area, maybe near the town of Watkins (now under Applegate Lake). It was held in the home's large attic, where one had to climb a ladder, as there were no stairs.

For some reason, I was the only child there, but I enjoyed the music and watching the dancing, which stopped when refreshments were served downstairs in the dining room. That was when I had fallen asleep, and my folks left me on a bench covered with their coats. I was terrified when I awoke and no one was in the room. Of course, everyone heard my distress, and Mother came climbing up the ladder to comfort me.

There was a neighborhood dance almost every month in someone's home, even one in the barn of my grandfather, Amos McKee. I was told it was in late spring, when the hay was gone. The barn had a good dance floor, probably on purpose, because it was rather common in those early days to have a barn for dancing. We had just moved into our newly built home near the Palmer Creek and upper Applegate River, around 1932, when Mother decided to have a home dance. My dad moved most of the furniture into the bedrooms, and for some reason, my fractious mother had the floor thoroughly scrubbed, even though it would later be covered with dancing powder. Even the windows were cleaned, which I don't think anybody noticed.

Mother spent much time that morning before the dance preparing refreshments for the midnight snack. In those days, the snack was more than just a little bite. She made large sandwiches of homemade bread filled with tasty ground-up baked chicken, accompanied with potato salad, deviled eggs, and a choice of burnt sugar or cream cakes for dessert.

My Grandma McKee had made phone calls on the "farmers only" phone line (formerly the Blue Ledge Mining line) to the neighborhood about the upcoming event. I remember a lot of high school kids came, probably because my brother and sister were of that age. It was in the summer, and those kids spent more time outside than inside for the dancing. The younger ones, my age, had a good time sliding up and down on the slick floor between dances. That was more fun that trying to dance.

We sometimes attended public dances at the Applegate Grange, and when the Upper Applegate Grange built their hall in 1936, well, that ended the home dances in our neighborhood. We were going to our Grange dances once a month. They were sometimes so crowded it was difficult to dance, but they were always enjoyable for seeing so many neighbors, friends, and relatives.

It is strange that I was never a good dancer. Probably being born with two left feet didn't help. My family tried to teach me the many dance steps, but nothing happened. So when I met my future husband and found he couldn't dance either, I was pretty happy.

A few years later my Aunt Clara Smith, my mother's sister, who was a very good dancer, started having square dances, which had become popular again. She and her husband, Rolland (Sandy), had purchased the Crump ranch at Little Applegate and Yale Creek roads. The abandoned Little Applegate School, still on the property at that time, was where the dances were held.

Our first time at those dances was when our daughter, Janeen, was about two years old. Aunt Clara insisted we come, even though there was not a place for little children, so we made a bed for Janeen on the back seat of our car and parked close to the front door. She was accustomed to sleeping there on our camping trips and soon fell asleep, probably helped by the sound of music.

A square dance required eight couples for two squares. If more couples came, turns would be taken so no one was left out. Sometimes there were not enough couples for a square, but that didn't keep folks from improvising their own dancing routine, which sometimes caused a lot of laughter.

There was no electricity, but the kerosene lights filled the room with a nice warm glow. Aunt Clara's old wind-up Victrola phonograph would play the square-dance records, and when the record began to run down, she would quickly run to rewind, then dash back to the square, rarely missing a beat. Everyone would laugh!

Toward the end of the evening, some people would be getting a little fatigued, especially my Uncle Sandy. He was a hardworking man with a work-clock-setting brain. His routine was: up at the break of dawn, a long day of work, then early to bed. So one night, when his dancing interfered with his bedtime, we actually witnessed him falling asleep, still standing, while his wife went to rewind the music.

I'm sorry that I can remember only a few who attended those dances. The ones I remember were Fred and Ethel West, Lance and Stella Offenbacher, Charles and Virginia Chittoch, and one time, Wayne and Jackie Reavis. There had to be more of the Little Applegate people and maybe some newcomers there. I just mostly remember what fun we all had.

My husband and I became expert square dancers, or so we thought. It was the only time we had the beat, the time, and the feet.

Leola Culy and Marguerite Watson dance at Southern Oregon Normal School, 1931. Southern Oregon University Hannon Library.

A Week of Chores

I think growing up without electricity was the most difficult when it came to washing our clothes, a chore that (naturally) fell to Mother, Gladys, and me. Mondays were wash day, and Mother would get up very early, fill the copper boiler with water, and begin heating it on the kitchen stove. She would add some lye and shavings from a bar of soap to the water, then the white clothing. The colored clothing was always done after the whites. The clothes were stirred for an hour or so with a cut-off broom handle, and then each piece of clothing was placed in a wash tub of warm water and scrubbed on a washboard using a bar of Fels Naptha soap. We would take turns with the scrubbing, but I still remember many finger blisters.

The clothes were wrung out by hand, sometimes taking two of us on one item. Mother eventually acquired a hand-turned clothes wringer that she attached to the rinsing tub. That was wonderful! Then the whites went into the "blued" rinse water. They were wrung again and taken to the clothesline to hang until dry. The clothes that needed starching were placed in a mixture of flour and water before we hung them on the line. We did all our cotton dresses, aprons, and men's shirts this way.

We had to arrange the clothing tastefully on the clotheslines. Mother did not want to see it any other way. Underclothes went on the middle lines where they could not be seen. All sheets, blankets, and quilts hung together. If the weather was bad, we hung everything on lines on our screened back porch.

Tuesday was our ironing day. We sprinkled the clothing with water the night before and rolled it up in bath towels to "cure." We built a very hot fire in the stove for the "sad" irons. When a drop of water on the iron hissed, the iron was ready to use. The heat was good for about three minutes; then the iron went back on the stove, where other irons were ready. A paraffin pad stayed on the ironing board for any iron that became sluggish from starch build-up. We could iron lightly over the pad to make the iron slick again. We had to be very careful not to over-use the treatment of paraffin or make a burned spot on the clothes.

Wednesday was usually bake day, especially for bread. It was always tricky getting the oven in the wood-burning kitchen stove to the right temperature. Many times the bread was ready for baking, but we would have to leave the oven door open until the oven cooled some. We did not have bread pans, so Mother would put the loaves together in one large baking pan. I liked this because there were only crusts on the tops and ends of each loaf. I was not fond of the crusts.

Saturday was definitely the day to clean house. Every inch had to be swept and dusted, windows washed, and the outside privy scoured with a broom dipped in lye water and part of a sack of lime dumped down the hole. This reminds me of another story which is better than cleaning.

The chickens in our flock kept pecking our Barbed White chicken on the head, threatening her life. I came to the rescue of "Isabelle" by keeping her in our fenced yard. She became my special pet, following me around like a dog. I began letting her go to the privy with me, and, to my delight and amusement, she would jump up on the seat to sit on the usual catalogue beside me. She would spend the time preening herself, and we would talk to each other. No one can believe what a chatterbox she was. I had her for quite a while until one day she disappeared. I was heartbroken. I waited for days for her return. Either she got outside of our yard where some varmint or hawk got her, or…she ended up in my mother's chicken noodle soup. My folks did think she was sort of a nuisance, especially her droppings on the walks and steps, which I had to clean. Whatever caused her disappearance, I missed my pet chicken.

Telephone and laundry services—two luxuries not available in the Applegate Valley. The Jacksonville Miner, January 4, 1935.

McKee Bridge Park

An early settler, James McLaren, sold two mining claims to Deb and Leila McKee in 1902, and the McKees built a two-story house on the east side of the Applegate River. They later ran a stage stop there for travelers going to and from the Blue Ledge Copper Mine. The McKee Bridge gets its name because Deb McKee donated the land it sits on. The bridge crosses the river just above a well-used camping area and swimming hole. Many a miner would camp there on his way to or from Jacksonville on a supply run. The bridge building crew also camped there and many times arranged to have their meals at the McKee stage stop.

At that time the road from Ruch to the Upper Applegate forded the river a couple of times, so spring travel was often difficult or impossible. Sometime in 1906 or 1907, Jackson County made a new road that stayed on the east side of the Applegate River, doing away with the river crossings. However, the Eastside Road at Dead Horse Hill was very dangerous, and with the increase of traffic, especially from the Blue Ledge Copper Mine in World War I, the county built two covered bridges. In 1917 the Cameron and McKee bridges were finished, and even though the road was not paved, travel to the Upper Applegate became much easier.

By the 1930s the spot was a well-established campground, according to the following article by Maude Pool in the *Medford Mail Tribune*: "Big Applegate, July 24, 1936. Camps Improved in Forest Areas: At the campground at McKee Bridge, already equipped with a pump, stone stoves, and tables, the hydraulic rams will be installed in the Applegate for irrigation of shrubbery, and a diving board will be erected. Dee Mills is in charge of this work. Both camps will be enclosed with a rustic pole fence, with cattle guards."

I remember some of my teenage friends came out one day to swim and spend the night. We were the only ones in the campground that night, and we felt as safe as if we were in our own homes. We had blankets and quilts on which to lie on the hard ground. By morning the ground seemed much harder, but that's the way it was—no luxuries.

Again from a *Tribune* article by Maude Pool, on August 4, 1939: "McKee Park Pool Will Be Lighted: McKee Bridge Forest Park, one of southern Oregon's most popular free resorts, will have its swimming pool in the Applegate River equipped with electric lights within a short time, according to local Forest Service officials. CCC workmen at Camp Applegate are constructing a water wheel which will be installed in a farmers' ditch running through the park. The wheel will operate a generator, and it is expected that the system will supply sufficient electricity for six lights at the pool. The work is under the supervision of H. Barnhart, project superintendent at Camp Applegate. An added improvement planned for the immediate future in the park is a sprinkling system to dampen the grounds. Three thousand feet of pipe have been purchased, and the water will be piped in, although its exact source has not been determined. It is thought probably that the Forest Service will enlarge the capacity of the park with the purchase in the near future of an adjoining half acre of ground."

I don't recall the swimming hole ever being lighted at night, as stated in the 1936 news clipping. However, the Forest Service did build a nice bathhouse for changing into swimsuits—one end of the building for women and the other for men. It was located on the bank near the ditch above the swimming hole. And at one time there was a children's playground with swings much larger than the usual size for school playgrounds. One could really fly high. Perhaps my fear of heights is why I don't remember there being a slide, but a cousin of mine says there was a fun one. The slide was made even more fun after he and the other boys used wax paper to make it really slick.

There also was a large teeter-totter that I rarely got on because I usually ended up being on the upper end of it. The thing I remember enjoying the most was the two "swinging benches" that held three people on each side. When the Grange had their dances, it was a place for teenagers to gather and chat during the night.

I also don't remember when the park became a day-use-only park, but I do remember Sunday afternoon trips to McKee Bridge Picnic Grounds as a favorite pastime for my family, who had little other entertainment in this neck of the woods.

Even our dog took advantage of the outing, although he was never really invited to go with us. That dog just happened to be there when we arrived and acted as though we were strangers to him. He would run away each time we tried to catch him. Other people must have thought we were trying to mistreat him, but the next morning he would show up for breakfast and was very happy to let us see all of the garbage he had dragged home from the park. We think he must have known when the weekends came, as he rarely strayed from our farm during the week.

Through the years many people have enjoyed the shade of the tall pines and the cool water of the deep swimming hole at the park. I am sure that it will continue to be a wonderful place where people can enjoy the Applegate River.

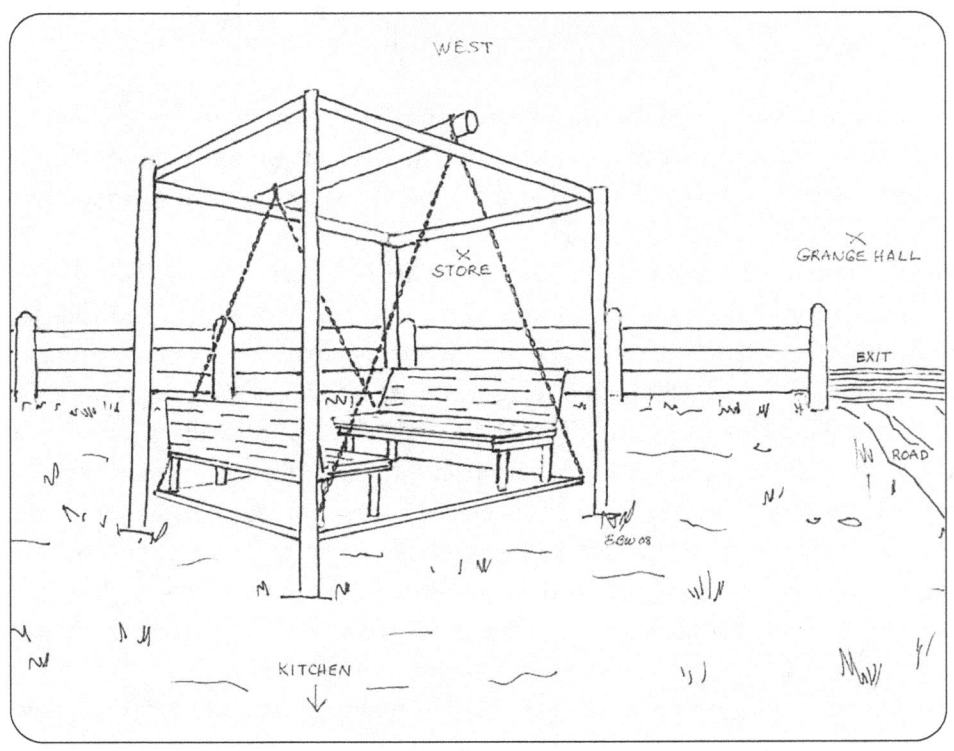

The old bench swing drawn by Evelyn Byrne Williams.

Fabric quilt block by Evelyn Byrne Williams.

Growing up on a Squirrel Ranch

I knew quite a few "squirrel ranchers" when growing up in the Applegate. My family was one of them, so I am quite qualified to clarify our status from the other kinds of ranchers and farmers here. Of course, the squirrel ranch name started because the disliked digger squirrels were already on the premises. There was no disgrace in living on such a place, but there was no income to be made from the squirrels. One could have some chickens, raise a garden, and grow some hay for a milk cow, as we did, but rich you would never be on the squirrel ranch.

In 1930, my dad started working for the Forest Service at Star Ranger Station, just during the summer months or fire season. For about ten years, he was either at a guard station or up on Tallowbox lookout, so Mother was left to run our ranch with the help of us children. I loved our squirrel ranch but hated the work. Everyone had to do his or her part. My brother, Morris, ten years older than me, and my sister, Gladys, eight years older, had learned to milk the cow. I decided I didn't want to learn to milk, and I didn't! At a very young age, I made up my mind that I wanted to live in the country, but not do farming or ranch work.

One of my favorite activities was fishing. Since we lived so close to the river, we had many fish dinners. Morris taught me all the fishing techniques, and we would have contests to see who caught the first, largest, or the most fish. Rainbow trout was our favorite.

Our dog, a shepherd we called Pat, also liked to fish. When he heard me getting my fishing pole from our back porch, he would go crazy with excitement. I had taught him to stay close beside me while I fished, and when I caught a fish, I would throw the line so the fish would land quite a ways behind us. Pat would run and jump on the fish, paws firmly keeping it there for me to remove the hook. He and I had many happy times together.

Horses and cows were not for me. One time when I was about seven, my grandpa, whose farm was on both sides of the Applegate River, was going to cross the river with his mower and team of horses on his way home from cutting hay all day. He had his derrick horse following in the back and wanted me to ride her across the river ahead of him. I told him I had never ridden a horse, and he said it was about time I did. He put me up on her bare back and handed me the reins. I grabbed her mane and we started across. The moss-covered river rocks were my undoing when she slipped and slid in midstream. Off I plunged into the water, madder than a wet hen. Grandpa was laughing at me as my horse went on across. I ran home and told Mother what Grandpa had done, and she only seemed to be relieved that I had not drowned.

I did like chickens. When Dad built our chicken house and Mother brought some baby chicks home, I was so excited. I helped with the feeding and watched the chicks grow up and start laying eggs. I never complained about helping with the monthly cleaning of the roosts and floors. We brushed Black Leaf 40 (nicotine) on the pole roosts to kill chicken lice and put fresh straw or hay on the floors. It was interesting to see how the chickens reacted to the cleanliness. They actually talked all about it while scratching the straw or hay and preening.

I liked gathering the eggs each evening from the nests at the far end of the building. Sometimes, a hen wanted to become a mother and refused to move from her nest of several eggs. I was happy if Mother gave me permission to let her stay there. I watched over the hen until the little chickens hatched.

In the mornings, Mother poured clabbered milk over the store-bought "chicken mash" she put in the feed boxes. Those chickens were as happy as kids at an ice-cream social. They hurriedly gulped it all down before spending the rest of the day outside, nibbling green grass, hunting bugs, and eating the crushed oyster shells needed for their digestive systems. However, outside there were hawks to fear, which could quickly swoop down and effortlessly grab a chicken, especially a small one, and sail off with it for a meal.

I never wanted to witness when it was time for a chicken to become a dinner or when all were past their prime. I usually made an excuse to go visit my grandma across the river. Later I would see some canning jars filled with those many chicken parts. I must admit, after some time, to liking the many meals of chicken noodles, dumplings, and soups from those dear chickens.

One day I came home from school with some leftover powdered poster paints that you could mix with water. I could hardly wait to get home to show my treasures to Mother. But she wasn't there, so I decided to go ahead and surprise her by painting the back of our chicken house with a mural in all those wonderful primary colors with some black and white mixed in. I climbed a ladder to start my masterpiece. I don't remember what I painted, but I know it was very bright and colorful. It was finished by the time I heard Mother coming in our car, and I could hardly wait for her happy reaction.

I think she almost had a heart attack when she saw my mural from Palmer Creek Road before driving down our driveway. As she got out of the car, there was a frown on her face, and I knew she was upset. She said my artwork could not stay there, so I had to get a bucket of soapy water and a broom to scrub it all off. She did lose her frown and, putting her arm around me, said it was a beautiful painting, but it was not for the chicken house that could be seen by everyone driving on our road. I still don't understand why it was so bad, but I am happy to say my artwork was never forgotten—a faint and spotty coloring remained on the old chicken house for many years.

Seems I have strayed from the squirrels, but I truly enjoyed the chickens on our squirrel ranch.

John Byrne milking a cow, a chore that daughter Evelyn chose not to learn at an early age.

Evelyn Byrne fishing on the Applegate River, one of her favorite "chores," with Pat the dog.

Shopping Trips to Medford

We planned a trip to Medford for shopping only a few times a year. I was allowed to go along, even if I missed a day of school. I could hardly get to sleep the night before due to my excitement and maybe a little trepidation, as the trip was long and I often became car sick on the way. No matter; I would never miss the excursion. My favorite trip would be in the fall before school started. I knew I would be getting a new pair of shoes, some school supplies, and if mother had enough money, a Milky Way candy bar.

We would park on Central Avenue within easy walking distance to all the stores. We always left the keys in the car, which you could not do today. The Buster Brown Shoe Store was one of the few places to go for my shoes. They had an X-ray machine set up so you could see your foot bones. This was very exciting for a country kid. Of course, that machine did not last long, as they found it to be dangerous to your health.

Maybe we would go to Newberry's, where mother bought fabric and other necessities. I remember being fascinated when the salesperson put mother's money in a small container and I watched it go on a line upstairs to a cashier, who sent back the change down the line. Mother always paid cash, as she had no checks, credit cards, or account at the store.

Another wonderful place was the grocery store, Gates and Lydiard. They had a lunch counter, and if Grandmother was with us, she would treat us to a bowl of soup and an ice cream dessert. I loved the canned vegetable soup then (not now), but the ice cream was the best. It was such a treat, as we only had it once or twice a year.

After eating we would sometimes go to a place near the lunch counter, which was carpeted and had comfortable chairs for people to rest in.

We usually saw someone we knew, especially from the Applegate. Mother and Grandmother would take time to visit, and then they would get busy with grocery shopping—100 pounds of flour, 50 pounds of white sugar, some brown sugar, large sacks of oats, some cornmeal, rice, a large box of soda, a can of baking powder, cornstarch, salt, a bucket of lard, maybe some spices such as pepper, cinnamon, ginger. We did not get canned food or fresh vegetables, except once in a while Grandmother would get a can of sardines, that being Grandfather's treat. If there were oranges or maybe bananas, we would get some.

One time I remember my mother going to the meat market and buying some bacon and treating me to a hot dog, which I had never eaten before. The butcher told us it was safe to eat even though it was cold. I enjoyed that cold hot dog, which really surprised my mother, since I was well known as a finicky eater.

When we had bought groceries and taken them to our car, we would drive around the block to the feed store to get some sacks of chicken feed and mash for the milk cow. Last, we might stop at Hubbards Hardware, and then we would pick up Grandpa. He would be waiting for us on Front and Sixth streets, after having done his own shopping—a supply of chewing and pipe tobacco and lunch with a "snort" of liquor at the tavern on Front Street.

I think I was about seven when I went to Medford with Mother and her friend, Mrs. Port. On our way home we stopped to see Molly Britt in Jacksonville. I had not been there before, so the unusual house with so much gingerbread trimming really fascinated me. I could hardly wait to see what was inside. I never dreamed I would be asked by Molly if I wanted to go upstairs to her father's studio while the adults visited.

Of course, I accepted the invitation, and she took me up the flight of stairs to enter her father's studio. I could not believe what I was seeing, a room so full of large photographs, paintings, and huge cameras. I knew Molly's father, Peter Britt, was the photographer who had taken many photos of my ancestors, probably with some of these cameras. However, I was more interested in the large portrait photographs and paintings. It took me a while to realize that many of the portraits were paintings and not photographs, this being the first time I had seen such. It was an experience I will never forget.

[Editors' note: Evelyn Byrne herself became an accomplished portrait artist in her adult life.]

Photo by Peter Britt of his home in Jacksonville, with son, Emil;
daughter, Mollie; and a friend on the porch.
Library of Congress Historic American Buildings Survey.

Peter Britt portrait of Charlotte Pence, Evelyn Byrne's maternal grandmother.

Peter Britt's artwork appears on the back of Charlotte's portrait.

From Home Improvements
to Indian Artifacts

Living in the Applegate was hard work. Dad built a chicken house and a barn with a woodshed attached. A lot of the framework for these buildings was of thick sturdy poles cut from trees within the area. He made shakes for the roofs from sugar pine trees. The woodshed was filled with dry wood and kindling that he would haul to the house in a wheelbarrow.

I remember one of the best Christmas presents I ever received was a little wheelbarrow that Dad made me from a wooden box and a wheel from my abandoned kiddy car. Mother painted it red, and I could hardly wait for Dad to fill it with kindling wood for me to haul to the wood-box at the house. How I wish I had kept that wonderful gift.

Mother worked hard, also. She made all of our dresses, aprons, coats, and most of our sleepwear. Weekly our kerosene lamp chimneys had to be cleaned, wicks trimmed, and the containers filled. There was a lantern for a nighttime trip to the privy or for Dad to use in the barn when he fed or milked the cow after dark.

One time mother bought an Aladdin Lamp that gave a much brighter light. It had a white web-like wick that was much easier to regulate for length. Dad liked the new light for his reading, which he enjoyed doing in the evening. Mother also found she could see much better for her sewing, but I no longer had the excuse of poor lighting for not doing my schoolwork.

Dad and Mother kept working on our house. The blankets and quilts we used for partitions were now gone, and new sheetrock paneling was installed. However, it was quite some time before the walls were finished, so some of the black tar paper used for insulation was still showing. We had to sweep it to remove the cobwebs and dust that frequently accumulated there.

Our water was gravity-fed to the house from a spring next to Palmer Creek. Mother was getting tired of the inconvenience of heating so much water for the washing and bathing, so Dad installed a tank in a corner of the back porch, connecting it to a pipe of coils in the fire box of the kitchen cook stove. Whenever the stove had a fire, we would have hot water. Mother also wanted to do away with the kitchen tub baths, so a shower (rather new for that time) was built in the bathroom. She then had a lavatory installed but no toilet because there was no septic tank. All the drain water was piped away from the house and drained over the bank.

As everyone knows, the Native Americans lived here before us, along the Applegate River. Many times when Dad plowed the garden, we would find arrowheads. Most were of black obsidian; some were red or white. The red and white ones were always small. Unfortunately, I do not know what happened to our collection. We probably gave it away. Little was thought about Native American history then.

One day my cousins and I found an Indian grave on our way home from school. The County had graded the road along our grandparents' field, cutting into the bank and exposing a skull. Naturally, it caused great excitement among us, and we started digging with hands and sticks. We soon tired and left the poor person's skull and some other bones still exposed. Then my cousin, Doug McKee, found a large obsidian arrowhead by the side of the road, and we became excited again at what more we might find. The next day after school, Walter Offenbacher, a classmate who lived near the Star Ranger Station, came with us to help finish the grave digging. Walter took home the skull and bones intending to put the skeleton together, but his horrified mother stopped him, and the bones soon disappeared from the household. I went back later to the grave site to get the many light blue and light pink beads, which I cleaned and sewed onto a pair of my homemade moccasins. Sadly they are long gone, and this many years later I have regretted the disturbance of that grave.

Applegaters shopped for home improvement supplies, and everything else, at Cap Ruch's General Store from 1897 to 1939.

Food Preservation

Nearly everyone living in the Applegate in the early 1930s had a farm animal or two, a vegetable garden, and possibly an apple tree. Many food items also came from the surrounding countryside. We hunted deer and bear, fished for trout, and harvested honey and other delectable foods. Preserving food for the coming winter was a hard and time-consuming necessity.

Sometimes my parents would arrange a camping trip to Huckleberry Mountain, with the goal of collecting and preserving huckleberries. (I do not remember exactly where this mountain is, but it may be near the Prospect area of the Rogue Valley.) My mother used a large copper boiler with a wooden rack inside to keep glass jars from resting on the bottom of the boiler and possibly breaking from the heat. My mother filled the boiler with water and berry-filled glass jars sealed with screw-on lids and rubber gaskets, then placed it over a fire and brought it to a boil.

Commercial pear orchards in the Rogue Valley also supplied fruit for canning. Many people, including my mother and me, would work at the packing house during the harvest season and take home rejected pears. One year my brother and mother were working at the packing house and sending home a lot of pears that my dad and I spent long hours cleaning and preserving. I don't remember having any fun doing that!

Another way of saving food for the coming winter was to dry it. We cut corn from the cob and placed the kernels on sheets laid on the roof of the house with sheer curtain material secured over the top. This allowed the air to flow through but kept the birds from eating the corn. Mother made a very good corn soup from the dried kernels.

Everything that could be pickled was. Pickled vegetables could be canned without the worry of botulism and made for some delicious eating. Of course, making dill pickles from cucumbers was common, but beets also were a favorite. Sugar is a great preservative, and many jams and jellies filled the cupboard in autumn. In earlier times a layer of hot beeswax or paraffin was poured on top of the cooked fruit in the jar, thus sealing in the flavor to be savored on a cold winter morning at breakfast.

Keeping food edible for a few days could be a challenge. Our family had a cold closet in the house and also used what we called a "California cooler." The closet was built into the house by leaving an opening in the floor and ceiling, then building a cabinet or closet over the openings. This allowed the cool air from under the house to circulate into the space. A screen was placed over the openings to keep out pests, and shelves were placed in the cabinet on which to set food. Pans of milk were kept in there—some to drink, others to be made into cottage cheese, or the cream skimmed off the top to make butter.

In summer, the California cooler was used outside, where the air would move through a screen of gunnysack material surrounding a wooden frame. On top of the frame was a wooden box for water with the ends of the burlap in it. The water would wick down the sides of the box, and the air moving through would cool the interior. A cool shady area in the yard made this an even more effective way of keeping our food cool.

Thankfully, today I use my freezer and refrigerator to keep food fresh or tastily preserved. However, it could be said that some of the flavors of the past are missed.

The boiler tub had many uses, such as canning and laundry (note the scrub board and bluing).

Old canning jar with rubber gasket and screw-on lid.

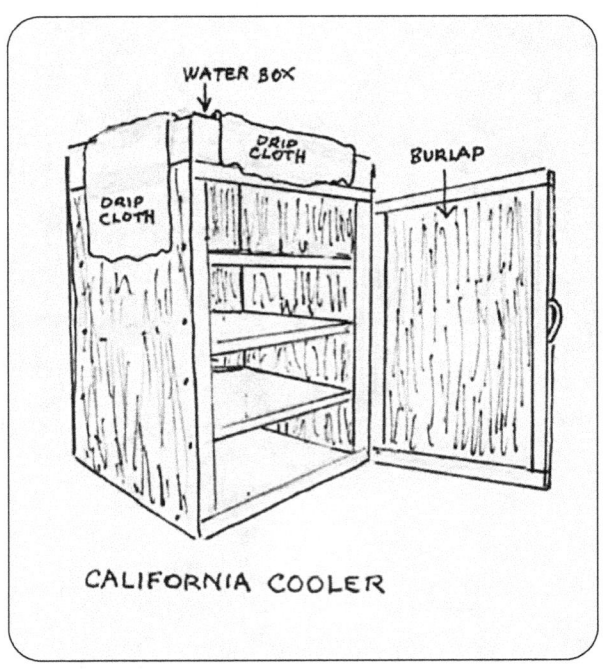

Summertime outdoor California cooler drawn by Evelyn Byrne Williams.

Learning to Sew

I was in sixth grade when Mrs. Maude Port (née Maude Agnes Peachey) came to our school and asked us girls if we would like to join a 4-H sewing club. Eighth grader Rosella Offenbacher and I were the only ones interested. We were invited to Mrs. Port's home at the Star Ranger Station, where her husband, Lee, was the ranger. Since my dad was one of the employees, I was well acquainted with the Ports and their son, Lee Jr., and daughter, Frances, both of whom had been classmates of my older brother and sister.

It was especially nice of Mrs. Port to offer sewing lessons because she was very involved in the community. Not only was she our school's clerk, but she was also an active member of the Upper Applegate Grange and a Home Extension participant. She admitted that after attending so many night meetings, she would become sleepy on her way home and have to pull over to the side of the road to take a short nap.

Rosella and I chose to make dresses for ourselves. Mrs. Port said that we should try something simpler because we were beginners. She suggested an apron, pillow, or laundry bag, but our hearts were set on dresses. She kindly gave in, warning us that it would be difficult and she would be disappointed if we did not complete the project.

It's strange that I do not recall if she took us to Medford for our patterns and materials, but I remember drawing a picture of what I wanted my dress to look like. Of course, it was not simple, but that dear lady probably feared she would lose my interest if she did not grant me my choice. Naturally, I chose a striped material, which only added to the difficulty of the project. I think my mother must have had a council with Mrs. Port to make sure I would finish that dress.

I don't remember how often Rosella and I went to Mrs. Port's for our instructions, but after school I would walk there, which was about four miles away. Our first meeting to cut out our dresses was very exciting. Mrs. Port did an amazing job of improvising my pattern from my drawing, and I thanked her for doing that. We then did all the necessary markings and pinned pieces together before basting with a needle and thread. Then it was time to hurry home to show Mother my accomplishment. After supper that evening, we lit a lamp so I could continue basting.

I also don't remember if Mrs. Port had a treadle or electric sewing machine or even if I used it. They did have a generator to use for lights at the station and their home, so it's possible that they had an electric sewing machine. I just remember her being pleased with my sewing that I did on our "Minnesota" treadle sewing machine. My mother was a good seamstress, and many times I had to rip out stitches after she examined my work. I almost gave up the dress-making project at times but did not want to hurt Mrs. Port's feelings, so I finished the dress.

I really liked Rosella's navy-style dress. I don't remember if our dresses were later displayed at the 4-H fair, but Mrs. Port was very proud of us and took our pictures. Rosella stood by a rose trellis on the left side of the Ports' home. My photo was taken by the steps near the road. Note the saddle shoes we both wore. One was not in style at that time without saddle shoes.

I regret never seeing Rosella again. She went on to high school, married, and a few years later, sadly, died of cancer. Often times now, when I pass the Star Ranger Station, I think about my many memories of her and Mrs. Port and the 4-H dressmaking project.

Rosella Offenbacher (left) and Evelyn Byrne (right) model the first dresses
they ever made during a 4-H sewing class taught by Maude Port.

To Victoria and Return, Part One

I found a few pages written by my dad about a trip my parents took in 1937 to Victoria, Canada. I do not remember my dad writing about this trip, but I do recall how unhappy my sister, Gladys, and I were to be left behind. My Uncle Harold, Aunt Maud, and their son, Bernard, were here from San Jose, and they planned to travel north to Victoria. With my parents and all their camping gear in the car, there was not enough room for Gladys and me, and, who knows, maybe it was just nice to have some time away from the kids.

I was 11, and I remember my Uncle Harold giving me a five-dollar bill for my birthday, which was the day after they left. Gladys, several years older, and I stayed at our house, though I did spend a lot of the time at my grandparents' place across the river. I ate with them and helped with the haying by making many trips with cold water to the fields where Grandpa was working.

Here are a few excerpts from my dad's notes, along with a photo. By looking at the clothing they are wearing, it's hard to believe they were camping along the way!

Dad's Story

So, the morning of the 21st of June 1937, found us trekking across the wire footbridge. Harold, impatient to be away, performed most of the menial labor, and when everything was beside the car, started stowing it away. It took a good deal of maneuvering and repressed swearing to get everything tucked in and our bed roll lashed on behind.

At this point Dad, who was mowing hay just over the wire fence, flushed a rabbit, and the dogs were in hot pursuit. Bernard hastily got his movie picture camera in position, and no doubt would have got a picture notable for its action, as the rabbit and dogs came right down the road and into the midst of us, then dashed away and out of sight. Later we learned that the film was stuck and did not register. But this put us in a good frame of mind, and we hurriedly bid the kiddies goodbye and were off. It flashed over me that we might not see them again—there are so many things that can happen—but this is life, and we put it quickly aside.

We went down the Applegate and were in Grants Pass at 10 am. The road between Grants Pass and Roseburg is noted for its crooks and turns, but the country is very beautiful, or at least it is at this time of the year. We were pretty well wedged in the back seat and did not slide around a great deal, but taking the turns at a pretty good clip, we imagined we could hear the car groan at every joint. Maybe it is just a Scotchy idea of ours not to want to subject such a fine piece of machinery to so much strain.

There also developed at this time the first faint rumblings of the back-seat drivers. It was destined to grow louder and more confusing when we reached the cities, but it seemingly was taken in good part by the drivers—or at least we hope it was.

We ate lunch in Roseburg at 12:30. Most notable through this section are the wild roses in bloom in fields and pastures along the highway. We noted cattle and sheep and rolling green hills. Arrived at Cottage Grove at 3:33 pm and visited Ernest and Allenne [Pearl's brother and sister-in-law]. We were in Salem at 6:20 and decided to camp. The Lone Star Auto Camp looked good, so we unpacked and later were directed to the "Argo" hotel, where we dined for fifty cents a plate, family style. As we had had a strenuous day, we retired early.

We had heard a great deal of the Columbia River highway, and we were not disappointed in the highway or in the grandeur of the scenery. Multnomah Falls has to be seen to be appreciated, and all of the falls along here would be a pleasant place to be on a hot day; one could easily take a cold shower from the spray. Numerous trails lead from here up into the back country, and we believe we could enjoy a few days following these trails out with a light camping outfit.

Hunger again assailed us, and we reached Bonneville dam in time for lunch. Plenty of eating places and good deal of a rush, as this is a busy place. The government has built a small town below the dam on this side of the river, presumably for government workers and officials. Numerous small houses are built in all the nooks and corners along the highway here. We drove on up a short distance to the Bridge of the Gods, a toll bridge, and crossed to the Washington side. This seemed to be the main town for the laborers. From an observation point we watched the huge machinery in operation. Towers, cables, cars, huge cranes, shovels, and mixers, and men crawling around like a lot of ants. We hope the power generated from this great dam will be used wisely and well for all the people.

Camas was our next stop. We were in a heavy downpour and pulled into a filling station and took a look at our bed roll to check the moisture. Here is a large paper mill; the attendant told us the largest of its kind in the world, but we don't know if this is correct. Vancouver, Washington, next, and then North again. Gassed up in Woodland, and then on to Chehalis, a very nice town. We did some shopping here, as we have a light camping outfit with us.

Sunup, about five o'clock, June 23, just enough to induce us to roll out early, and then it started raining again. We were equipped with a waffle iron, and although it was against the rules in all the camps we visited, we plugged it in and started making waffles. It seemed like pouring sand in a rat hole, but Harold stayed manfully with it until we were all fortified for a day's run.

At 11:30 we found ourselves in a large public market [Seattle], and as the waffles and coffee seemed to have lost their potency, we dined, overlooking the bay or sound. This is a very large market, and everything looked good. Wanted to buy some strawberries and kept looking the stalls over. Harold wanted to boycott the Japanese, of which there were a goodly number, so we finally bought some from a white dealer, but when we emptied them out that evening, the bottom ones were small and moldy. Ahem!!

The nicest gardens we saw on the trip were just south of Seattle. Left Seattle at noon and it is still raining. A wonderful new highway north to Everett. Stopped a few minutes in Everett at 12:45 and Bellingham at 2:30. This is all very rich looking farming country through here. We are now nearing the border, and this is one of the high spots of our trip, as we are about to leave the United States. We checked though at 3:30.

To be continued...

Left to right: Dad and Mom (John and Pearl Byrne) and Aunt Maud.

To Victoria and Return, Part Two

John and Pearl Byrne have been traveling north from the Applegate area to Victoria, Canada. The year is 1937, and they have been car camping along the way and enjoying the company of John's sister, Maud; her husband, Harold; and their son, Bernard. We join them again as they contemplate crossing the border into Canada.

Dad's Story, Part Two

One of the Canadian officials was a little officious and reprimanded Harold for not having his papers with him. Said he might not be able to get back into the U.S. without them. It made us some uneasy, but we decided to smuggle Harold back over the border in some manner regardless of the cost. On all our trip we were treated very courteously by everyone.

A short distance north of the line we encountered several small stands close to the highway, all selling native honey. Pint and quart containers stacked up in pyramids, and it looked inviting, so we bought some. The young man selling said it was of native production, and we found it to be very nice tasting honey.

We began to sit up and take notice, as we are now in Canada. Crossed the Fraser River and reached New Westminster at 4 pm. Another nice little city. Camped at "Hollywood Auto Court" about eight miles this side of Vancouver. The cabins were modern and the prices reasonable, although they were due for a raise July 1. Supper over we drove into Vancouver, this stretch of highway being called the "King's Way." Vancouver claims a population of 246,000. We had intended doing more cooking on the trip, but the women are lying down on the job, and the men voted a sit-down strike, so we dined at the "White Lunch."

What one notices most in Vancouver are the cars and the people. The city seems to be several years behind the U.S. Lots of small cars of old vintage and the trucks also. They must use a great deal of sawdust and coal, as we saw a lot of this being transported in sacks loaded on open trucks. The people are typically English as far as we are able to judge, and it seemed off to see so many people of our type. We were told that Victoria was more English than Vancouver, but we were unable to see much difference.

Drifting around the city, Harold, who was the brains of the party, this day conceived the idea of following one of the sightseeing busses, which proved very satisfactory. Bernard maneuvered in behind one of the busses leaving at 2 pm, and we followed it all the way through Stanley Park, making a complete circle. At Prospect Point work is under way to build a bridge across Burrard Inlet to North Vancouver. Looking northeast across the inlet, one can see North Vancouver and a beautiful array of high mountains, rivers, and inlets, a very enticing picture to a hunter or fisherman. These parks are all beautiful, and it is useless to try to describe them.

We traveled east, then north, and then gradually turned south, where we could look out across the channel to Vancouver Island. At this point another halt was made at a tea garden. We pulled ahead of the bus and waited, viewing a monument erected to the memory of Captain Fraser. We did not know just where the bus was going next. When the bus pulled out, the driver gave us several lusty toots of the horn, whether it was in salute or derision, we do not know, as anything might be thrown at a car bearing a California license. Ahem!

We wound around through a maze of beautiful homes, flowers, hedges, and lawns, as there are a lot of retired and wealthy people in Vancouver. Back in the city we took in a show at the Century Theater. When we came out it was 8 pm, and the sun looked to be still about a half hour above the horizon. We are far enough north that the days are pretty long. We stayed at our same camp and "500 rummy" was enjoyed until a late hour. This developed into somewhat of a cutthroat game, and we ourselves were most always in the hole. Sometimes from a dead silence the word "rummy you" would be shouted from our lusty throats, and the occupants of the adjoining cottage would turn over with a groan, as in some of these cottages, a thin partition separates the two, with a garage on each side. Anyway, they were Californians, or most of them were, and were used to disturbances.

We boarded the "Princess Victoria" and were off for Nanaimo at 11 am. Large rafts of logs are in evidence, and one gets a better view of the country above North Vancouver. The trip across was pleasant, but uneventful, reaching Nanaimo, a city of 7,000, at 1:30 pm. There was something peculiar about the name of this city, and every time we tried to pronounce it, everyone tried, until it became a joke. We lunched at Shasta Café at 2 pm, and headed north over a good paved highway. Passed through Wellington, a large coal-mining district.

June 28. The weather warm and clear again this morning. Headed for Butchart's Gardens, located several miles northeast of the city. Passed a large observatory but did not feel like spiraling up to it. After winding around through some low hills we made a sharp left-hand turn, then went down into a parking court. We noticed one officer here, but on our return he was gone. We were allowed to wander at will about the gardens without attendant.

To describe these gardens would be impossible. The sunken part of the garden is an immense mined-out quarry. From an observation point you look down into a mass of flowers and shrubbery. The erosion on the rocky sides of the walls has allowed the flowers to grow in profusion aided by frequent rains. Strips of green lawn and masses of flowers of every description. The air is heavy with the odor, and we could almost feel the thousands of honeybees struggling upward to some hives we saw later. We sure would like to taste some of that honey.

Up early June 29. The weather is a bit cloudy. We boarded the S.S. Iroquois at 9:15 am and are off for Port Angeles. Bernard got some more pictures, leaving the docks and an aeroplane passing us, skimming low to the water. This is quite a little trip, and one gets the swell of the ocean. We began to feel rather peculiar so went inside and sat down as near the center of the boat as possible and practiced rhythmic breathing. This helps a lot if you know how it is done, and one would look so undignified leaning over the rail. Pearl had a Calvin Coolidge look on her face, and Maud sort of a do-or-die. Maud and Bernard finally made a hasty trip out on deck, but we did not follow. They probably were looking at the scenery.

And finally: We are getting back to the crooked highway (Roseburg and south), but there is a good deal of historic interest here in all these placer streams and mountains. Occasionally you catch glimpses of the old road and can visualize a team and wagon bumping and grinding around a narrow mountain road. It is certainly a long step from those days to our present mode of travel.

Grants Pass seems to be the tourist city of them all. The whole of Sixth Street is turned over to the tourists' parking, and you can leave your car parked here all day if necessary. We lost track of our timetable here, but it is some time in the afternoon, and we are headed toward home. The Applegate country looked very good, and the outline of the blue Siskiyous looked inviting. At odd times, for amusement, we have looked over maps of this country, of Canada, of Alaska, and we have a great desire to see them at close range, but we believe if we ever had the good fortune to do this, there would come a time when we would be glad to come home.

[Note from Janeen Sathre: John Byrne has been gone for over 40 years (he died in 1977), but this wonderful story of a cherished trip he took so long ago keeps him a part of our family—his children, grandchildren, and great-grandchildren.]

At Butchart Gardens: (L to R) Aunt Maud, Dad (John Byrne),
Uncle Harold, Mom (Pearl Byrne).

Fir Glade Guard Station

In the early 1930s, the Forest Service had several guard stations in the back country of the Applegate River. These stations might be along the route used to carry supplies to the fire lookout towers or in areas hard to reach on short notice where a crew of firefighters could stay. One of the most interesting to me was at Fir Glade, near Whisky Peak and its lookout tower.

In 1939 my newly married brother, Morris, and sister-in-law, Florence, were stationed at Fir Glade by the Forest Service. My mother decided to arrange a trip there to visit them. She invited my former sixth-grade teacher, Bertha Haskins, and husband, Wallace, as well as my seventh-grade teacher, Doris Work, to go along. Mr. Haskins had grown up in the Applegate and had been to Fir Glade several times. This was a chance for him to show his wife, who was from Illinois, our Oregon environment.

In the early morning we drove a short way from Copper (now under the Applegate Lake) to the Middle Fork, where the road ended. We met Melvin Arnold, the Forest Service packer, at the trailhead there. He had a horse and a mule loaded with supplies headed for Fir Glade and the Whisky Peak Lookout. We were going to spend the night, so I carried my things in a flour sack. Backpacks in those days were made for men, and the wooden frames covered in canvas were quite heavy when fully loaded.

For most of us there was much excitement for this first-time trip to Fir Glade. We anticipated a good meal that evening with Morris, Florence, and my sister, Gladys, who had gone to Fir Glade a week or so ahead with a Mr. Knudson, who also was packing supplies to Whisky Peak. He asked her if she would like to go on over to Frog Pond, where Knox McCoy lived. She said she would be glad to see Mr. McCoy, who often times had stopped at our parents' home on his way to get his supplies for winter. He would spend the night in the barn, have breakfast with my parents the next morning, and put baby Gladys on his knee to play horsey.

It didn't take long for the miles to take their toll. I ran out of steam after foolishly walking too fast at the beginning. Bertha Haskins developed blisters on her heels, so Mr. Arnold let her ride his horse. By day's end she had saddle sores, too. We really felt sorry for her, but she did not complain, being a good sport. We were so glad when the picturesque setting of Fir Glade came into our view.

The log cabin, I believe, was built by area cattlemen who would bring their cattle up into the high country in the summer to eat the grasses in the many alpine meadows. The cabin's large open front faced a meadow with a slow stream flowing through it, and the back was shaded by big fir trees. I don't recall what we had for supper that night, but I do remember the delicious applesauce Florence made from the apples that Mr. Arnold brought her.

Those apples grown in the upper regions of the Applegate were known for their unusual tart-and-sweet flavor. They were extra-large and mid-green. Most people in the area grafted a branch from the original tree onto their own apple trees. My mother said it was called the Watkins apple, which probably came from the early pioneer Watkins family. My family considered it the best apple they ever had. Too bad that the trees were probably destroyed when the Applegate Lake was being built.

Where and how we all slept at Fir Glade that night, I do not remember. There were no sleeping bags or air mattresses as there are today. Mr. Haskins and my brother may have cut some fir boughs on which we placed our blankets. That was much better than sleeping on the bare ground. We did wake up very early the next morning because everyone was chilled. There is always a heavy cold dew in the high mountains.

After a hearty breakfast it was time to prepare for the return trip. After packing up that morning, I spent some time viewing the many names carved and written on the upper logs in the interior of the cabin. Needless to say, I just had to add mine.

Interestingly, my future husband, Clarence, spent time at Fir Glade when he worked for the Forest Service fire crews in the summer of 1946. They stayed about a week doing trail work and removing phone lines that ran from the guard stations to the lookouts.

Several years ago, I returned to Fir Glade with my daughter, Janeen, and her hiking group. It brought back such fond memories even though the cabin was gone. Some of the roof lies in a mass of weeds. Those logs with the names would have been such a keepsake. As I stood there looking at the meadow, I was glad it had not changed much, though time has taken its toll. All of those people mentioned back there in 1939 are gone except Gladys, teacher Miss Work, and me.

Gladys leading Fir Glade mules.

Whisky Peak Lookout.

Wallace Haskins, Evelyn, Florence, Morris, Gladys, Bertha Haskins, Pearl, and Doris Work (surname "Byrne" unless otherwise noted.)

Fir Glade cabin.

The 1939 Golden Gate International Exposition and My Grandmother, Katie Byrne

I was 13 years old when my family planned to attend the 1939 Golden Gate International Exposition, a World's Fair in San Francisco that celebrated, among other things, the city's two new bridges. I had not been that far away from home before, so the trip was very exciting to me, especially the visit to our relatives living near there. I would be seeing my paternal grandmother, Mary Catherine (Katie) Byrne, whom I had not seen in ten years.

Of course, we needed a bigger and better vehicle in which to make that long journey, as there were six of us going: my parents; brother, Morris, and his wife, Florence; my sister, Gladys; and I, plus our luggage. Mother had purchased the car in the summer of 1939, while Dad was still posted on Tallowbox Mountain, the Forest Service's fire lookout. He trusted her in doing such an important task, and she came home with a used 1935 V8 Ford sedan, all shiny, a dark-tan color with black fenders. Gladys and I said it was the "cat's meow," an expression commonly used then.

Preparations for appropriate clothing kept mother busy at her sewing machine, making our dresses. I got a wonderful coat with a real fur collar, a hand-me-down from an older girl cousin.

By the first part of October, Mother had everything ready for the exciting trip. So much of this has escaped my memory, especially where our luggage was put. That is a mystery. There was no trunk for it, and I know it was not on top of our vehicle, so it must have been secured to the back with the spare tire.

We left October 19 in the wee hours of the morning. Morris was the driver, with our parents in the front seat and Florence, Gladys, and me in the back. For some reason, I recall little of that long ride. It's strange that I don't remember stopping for lunch or points of interest along the way. The only part I remember well is seeing all those many distant city lights when arriving late that night at Pinole, California, where Dad's sister, Stella; her husband, Emmett O'Brien; and Grandma Katie lived.

The next day, I spent much time getting reacquainted with my grandmother. She had come to visit us for a time when I had my third birthday. She gave me a doll buggy and a small table with two chairs and teacups. (I still have them.) Because tea was her favorite beverage, we had tea parties at that table. Mother said I became terribly spoiled by Grandmother during that visit. I remember being so impressed with her very thick white hair coiled on top of her head—the most hair I had ever seen.

Days at Pinole went by with much visiting. Then we went to San Jose, where Dad's sister, Maud, and husband, Harold Watson, lived. On October 26, they escorted us to the fair on Treasure Island, which was built specifically for the exposition. I know we saw many interesting things so new to us. Mother enjoyed the Singer Sewing Machine exhibit and was given an attachment for making rugs on the sewing machine. The only problem was she just had an old treadle Minnesota machine, and it would not accept the rug maker.

I was more interested in the outdoor artist doing quick pastel landscape paintings, and I begged Mother for one. I know the price must have been low because she bought me one. Sad to say, after many years it disappeared from our household, probably because it was never framed.

Time has taken its toll on my memory, so these are just bits and pieces of that delightful trip and time spent with those dear relatives, back in time.

Left to right: Uncle Emmett O'Brien, Grandma Katie Byrne, John Byrne, Aunt Stella O'Brien, Aunt Maud Watson, Gladys Byrne, Florence Byrne, Pearl Byrne, Evelyn Byrne (and her coat with the fur collar), and Uncle Harold Watson.

Early Phone Service in the Applegate

There is no stopping progress, even for an old-timer like me. I didn't think I would cave in and get a cell phone, but I did. I use it for emergencies; however, I haven't given out the phone number as I probably would not answer a ringing purse. Sometimes new inventions take me a while to adjust to – like the phone service in the Upper Applegate.

When I was about 13, several farmers in the area were able to get what had been a private phone line extended from Jacksonville to the Blue Ledge Copper Mine, several miles south of Applegate Lake. This service provided enough line for 20 phones. Since my McKee grandparents lived along the main road, they were one of the lucky ones to be hooked up to the new party line. It seems to me that their ring was two long and one short. I am not really sure, but I do remember that the most important ring was 12 short ones. This was used for emergencies such as fire, accident, birth, or death—or to alert everyone that the game warden was on his way to catch someone with illegal meat.

Since we lived on the other side of the river from my grandparents, we would have to cross the river on a foot bridge and walk the quarter mile to their house with a message for my grandmother to call someone. I remember doing this many times, always with great excitement to be able to listen to her conversations with someone on the other end of the line.

It was not polite to listen in on a private conversation, but you knew when someone was doing it. Most times you could hear them breathing. If it got too annoying you asked them to please get off the line, and they usually did. Of course, there was no way of knowing who the eavesdropper was, but I know Grandmother listened in on conversations when she knew a neighbor had been sick or something important was happening. Also, if you knew that a neighbor was gone and their ring was heard, you would answer and take a message to deliver when they returned.

The phone was a great addition to the community. People could visit without having to walk miles. And it may even have saved lives, since a call could be made to the doctor who would be on his way out long before a person could arrive in town to summon him.

Even a good thing can have its problems. An interview by the Southern Oregon Historical Society with Guy Watkins, another old-timer from this area, tells about a telephone incident at Joe Bar, a supply center and "jumping off" place on the way to Blue Ledge Mine. It seems that two Swedes who lived across the creek from each other spent a lot of time arguing, to the point that they would cut each other's phones lines. One day when one of them was doing this, the other came storming out of his house and stood beneath the pole pointing his 30-30 at his neighbor. The man up the pole kept yelling for his mining partner to help and not to waste time going around to the bridge, but to wade straight across the creek as fast as he could. What happened then Guy did not say, but apparently no one was shot. Guy said it got a lot of laughs.

The phone became a personal thing for me when my uncle, who worked for a phone company in San Jose, California, brought us some old phones that had been replaced with newer models. He installed a private "pony" line from my grandparents' house to ours, to my uncle's, and to my brother's about three miles away. Now we could call my grandmother, our personal central, to pass on messages and receive them. We also could talk to my uncle and brother over our own phone line.

When my grandparents got a battery radio, my grandmother loved listening to a soap opera about poor old "Stella Dallas." Grandma would take her valuable time to sit and listen each weekly morning and then call my sister and me to relate the latest happenings. We were as eager as she was to find out what was going to happen to the poor soul. It did not take much to entertain us in those days. My mother was never interested in hearing about the episodes—I guess she had enough to worry about in those Depression years and did not need to hear about another's trials and tribulations.

My mother, who lived to be 101, saw more changes in her lifetime than any generation before. Beginning with the horse and buggy, she lived to see telegraphs, telephones, automobiles, airplanes, radio, television, medical wonders, submarines and ocean exploration, Sputnik, missiles, atomic bomb, man on the moon, personal computers, and the cordless phone. Someday my grandchildren may want to hang my cell phone, soon to be obsolete, on my antique wall phone and perhaps think about how it really was back in time.

The McKee house was one of the first homes to receive phone service in the Upper Applegate.

Joe Bar supply center and "jumping off" place on the way to Blue Ledge Mine.

The Forest Service Guard Station
near Yale Creek and Little Applegate

I remember the excitement in visiting my father, John Byrne, at his summer Forest Service Guard Station camp, where he was posted during fire season in the early 1930s. It was located on the former Harold Crump ranch, near Yale Creek, which flows into the Little Applegate River. The Forest Service chose to place its encampment near the bridge which crosses the Little Applegate River. It was a shady place and pleasant for summer living, though my father was not happy about being away from home and living the bachelor's life.

The shelter consisted of a wooden platform, about twelve feet square, with a framework on it, over which a canvas was stretched and secured. A table which also served as a desk held a Forest Service telephone. A bed and a straight-backed chair completed the furnishings. Nails driven into the wooden studs held my father's clothing.

Duty with the Forest Service required a uniform. This posed a problem for a family with no money and the country in the grips of the Great Depression. Fortunately, my father's brother-in-law was gainfully employed by the telephone company in San Jose, California. He agreed to loan my father some money. With that money Dad purchased several uniform shirts, a tie, and a hat, but no trousers, which were quite expensive. Those would be made from a riding skirt left over from my mother's horseback riding days. As luck would have it, the skirt just happened to be the right color of wool material. (Imagine having to wear wool in the summer!) My mother's brother, Floyd McKee, gave my mother a pair of his well-worn uniform pants from World War I. Taking them apart for a pattern was no small task, but what followed was even more demanding. After the tedious cutting out and sewing, the calf-length, tight-legged trousers needed a great number of buttonholes. I remember my mother doing these by hand for many nights with only the light from a kerosene lamp. Her maternal grandmother had been quite a professional seamstress, so mother had been properly schooled in tailoring. I wondered, even then, why those buttonholes needed so much attention, as they would be covered by the required leather leggings, another hand-me-down from Uncle Floyd's uniform.

My father looked sharp in his new uniform. I recall he kept those trousers on hand only to wear for an occasional inspection visit from Ranger Lee Port, who didn't follow protocol too much, anyway. I doubt anyone knew Dad's pants were handmade; besides, survival in those days meant one had to be thrifty and a "Jack of all trades."

The shoes Dad wore with his uniform also had to pass inspection. Since the purchase of new ones was out of the question, Dad resoled and polished his old ones. He was the family cobbler and kept all the family shoes wearable for as long as possible.

On the day he was to leave for the Little Applegate camp, my mother, the family barber, gave him a haircut. She then packed his clothes, food, and other essentials for his long stay during the summer. She was left to go on alone without her husband's help, but my brother, Morris, and sister, Gladys, who were much older than I, did help with milking the cow and other chores. I refused ever learning to milk a cow.

I was at the age when I would rather have gone and stayed with my father. I thought his camp was so inviting. It would be fun to do the cooking outside on a typical miner's wood stove and sit at a campfire in the evening while having a game of cribbage with Dad. I envisioned a summer of no chores if I stayed there, without my mother telling me to "get busy." Little did I realize how much work there was to keep wood for the stove and carry water in a bucket from the stream. Of course, the life of ease and fun for me, with Dad at the station, was not to be. However, I remember how joyful it was when my mother and I stayed overnight with him one time.

The Forest Service Guard Stations were equipped with the necessary tools for fighting fires. When a Guard received a call about a fire in his vicinity, his first response was to get to the scene as quickly as possible and then attempt to make a line around the fire with his shovel and Pulaski (a combination ax and pick). If he had an ax and saw with him, he could help contain the fire further by removing more fuel. Often he was on his own for containing the fire. Especially when there were other fires in the area, help could be scarce and miles away. When we knew my father was on a fire, we worried constantly until we knew he was safely back at his camp.

My high-school-age brother, Morris, had worked long enough to purchase an old Model T from Mr. Nichols, a nearby neighbor. It took quite some time for Morris to get the car in working order. When he finally did, the car was loaded with food and supplies for us to take to Dad at the Guard Station. There was only room for two people in the "T," so I got to go, and Mother stayed behind. I felt very privileged and excited about this excursion, as we rarely left our ranch. Our trips to Medford only happened a few times a year. "Dad will really be surprised to see us," Morris said as we waved good-bye to our mother and drove away.

Well, about a half-mile down the road from home near the Upper Applegate River, there was a very steep incline, a place the locals called the "dug road" because each winter the river flooded and washed the road out, and new dirt had to be dug for filling. We were almost to the top when the car refused to go any further. Morris backed the "T" quite a ways down the hill before making another racing attempt to reach the top. Again, the "T" sputtered to a stop. After about a dozen runs at the hill, my brother, cussing all the way, turned around and went home. I cried all the way back, while my older brother taught me a new vocabulary. We were met by a very disappointed mother. I don't recall what happened to the old "T," but I do remember that Morris later learned that he could have made it to the top of the incline if he had backed all the way up in reverse. It had something to do with the flow of gas. Some time later he purchased a little cherry red Chevy coupe, which I learned to drive, around and around in our hay field. It had no problem going up the incline of the dug road.

I think Dad was at the Guard Station on the Little Applegate for several years. Later he was stationed at Tallowbox Lookout and at the Thompson Creek Guard Station. Then he helped train young men in firefighting and took them to fires in the district until becoming a Forest Service Fire Inspector for logging operations here in the Applegate River District.

Later, my mother's sister, Clara (McKee) Smith, and her husband, Rolland, bought the Crump Ranch, so my family visited there quite often. Crossing the Little Applegate always brought back memories of my father's camp. I'm sure he and my mother thought of those as hard times, but I only remember them as good ones. Even now as I cross the bridge and see the overgrown willows, with the tall weeds and grass covering the ground, I get a lump in my throat, remembering that little camp where my dad stayed. My friend Colista (West) Bailey remembers stopping there one time with her grandmother, Ina Pursel, who gave Dad some garden vegetables or fruit. Perhaps Colista, my sister, Gladys, and I are the only ones left who remember that long-ago camp.

John S. Byrne (1887-1977).

John Byrne with shovel, placer mining
with cousin Patrick Foley.

Going, Going, Gone:
Some Old Buildings of the Past

I am so very fortunate to have been associated with two wonderful teachers who, after retiring, wrote fabulous books about our local history. One was Marguerite Black's *Ruch and the Upper Applegate Valley* (1990), and the other was Margaret Nesheim's *One Hundred Twenty-Three Years Search for Community* (1979). The latter book is about the schools in Jackson County.

I was also doing my own search for photographs of old buildings and pioneers in the Applegate Valley as inspiration for oil paintings I was working on. *[Editors' note: Evelyn, a well-known local artist, owned the Lamplight Gallery in Jacksonville for many years.]* Marguerite Black and I happily shared our collections as we canvassed the Applegate Valley. All this made us realize how very few old Applegate buildings are left, some dating back as far as the late 1800s and early 1900s. Each has a story from the past to tell, and some, hopefully, a future. As Margaret Nesheim said about one of them in her book, "Too many of the precious structures of the past have been destroyed. Perhaps, somehow, this one may survive."

As far as I know, the only old school building left from the 1800s in the Applegate Valley is the Forest Creek School. My dad started his first grade there. Fortunately, it has been saved by becoming a private residence of the Meeds family. The school was organized in 1878. Before that there was one at Logtown built in 1854. Margaret Nesheim had this to say about a famous student who went there: "Benjamin Franklin Irvine, the blind editor of the *Oregon Journal*, attended school at Logtown." His father was a miner on Jackass Creek, now known as Forest Creek.

Not far from Forest Creek, on the way to Jacksonville, there is a little old cabin that at least five generations of my family have passed by these many years. It has been said that this 1800s building was the home of Mr. Pryor Eaton. My mother, who was born in 1894, said her father often stopped there to rest the horses pulling a loaded wagon of dried Mexican beans to sell in Jacksonville. It is amazing that this old building is still there and looking the same today as it did then. "Perhaps this one may survive."

The house built by Cap Ruch in 1912 is the only survivor of old buildings in Ruch. At one time, next to this house, there was a Ruch store with a post office and a dance hall, which also served as a polling place. My parents attended a dance in that hall on their way home from their marriage in 1914.

Just past Hamilton Road, on Highway 238, there is an old house built in 1916 by William and Emma (Law) Smith. In later years, Emma built a second story on the house. Thankfully, the new owners built behind the old house, leaving a piece of Applegate history standing.

On down Highway 238, about halfway to Applegate from Ruch, another early 1900s house was built by Fred and Carrie (Cameron) Offenbacher. It was larger than most of the other homes being built in the Applegate. It is a two-story white house close to the road across from Long Gulch. The Offenbachers were well-known, productive farmers, and the house is still owned by some of their descendants.

Then on Hamilton Road is the James and Maggie (Riley) Buckley house, built in the 1880s. The first house they built there was destroyed by fire. The wood-framed antique water tower nearby is a classic structure that gives the house so much character. The couple had seven children, but few descendants followed to keep the land. They did, however, generously donate land for the Cantrall Buckley Park. Interestingly, a 1901 photograph taken near this house, of baseball players and picnickers, was used as a clothing guide for the 1973 Universal Studios movie, *The Great Northfield Minnesota Raid*. A scene in the movie, of a baseball game and picnic, was even filmed on this ranch.

The only old Uniontown structure left is a house built by Zack Cameron in the 1870s. It is located on Upper Applegate Road fairly close to the entrance of Little Applegate Road. This house is close to the road but cannot be seen because of a high pole fence erected several years ago. Mr. Cameron's wife was Rena (Verena) Kubli of Missouri Flat. He did some farming and helped in the Uniontown store, which was owned by a brother. Their one daughter had no children, and so the house passed out of the Camerons' possession.

I'm sure there are some other old structures in our Applegate that I have missed, but I would hope those mentioned here will continued to be saved for future generations to see.

"These old buildings do not belong to us only…they have belonged to our forefathers and they will belong to our descendants unless we play them false. They are not…our property, to do as we like with. We are only trustees for those that come after us."
William Morris, 1889

Forest Creek School, 1906.

68

Fred and Carrie Offenbacher's house, on today's Highway 238, early 1900s.

James and Maggie Buckley's house, on Hamilton Road, 1880s.

Bridges over the River

At one time the trails and eventually the main roads in the upper Applegate area were on the east side of the Applegate River. People living on the west side had to find ways to cross the river to reach trails and roads. Most of the time you could ride a horse or wade across the river at a ford, where the water was shallow and slow, but when the river was flooding, it would be impossible to cross anywhere. Thus, many forms of bridges sprang up along the river.

One of the most interesting bridges was the "swinging" footbridge made with fence wire, cables, and really snazzy planks of wood placed along the bottom. This contraption would be anchored on large trees several feet above the river, where winter floods could not reach. The photo of the bridge to Watkins School, from around 1891, shows one of these bridges with some children from the Watkins School standing on it. This bridge is now under Applegate Lake.

The Collings family, on the west side, had a walk-across bridge made of lumber, spanning from shore to shore just a few feet above the water. This bridge was used when the river was at its lowest. The Collingses would remove it when the water started rising and find other ways to cross to the west side. Now these areas are all under the Applegate Lake.

When community members organized the Beaver Creek School in 1898, they built a box-type conveyance so that children living on the opposite side of the river from the school could get to school. Cables held the box above the river, and the occupants would pull themselves across by hand. The school was on the west side and was sometimes called the McKee School because most children attending the school were from the McKee families. In 1913 a new school was built on the east side near what is now the Jackson Campground.

I don't know when the swinging bridge was built across from my home, about a mile upriver from the Beaver Creek School. I remember it was there in 1930, when our home was built near it on the west side. My family was happy for a shortcut to go visit my McKee grandparents, who lived across the river. The bridge was used all the time by my family and visitors, going to school or work and just because.

We encountered many obstacles as we crossed those swinging bridges, especially while carrying a lunch pail and some books on the way to school. We had to steady ourselves with a hand on the wire cable to keep from stepping off the 12-inch-wide boards. And, of course, it was called a swinging bridge for a very good reason—it could start swinging the minute you put your feet on it. It was extra scary when there was snow or ice on the boards. Dad would shovel the snow off, and I would put some of his wool socks over my shoes, to help to keep the bridge from being so slippery.

When better bridges allowed wagons and cars to cross the river in several places on the main road to the upper Applegate, the old way of crossing was no longer needed. Many of those old bridges became dangerous, and one by one they were taken down. The last time I saw the swinging bridge by my home was in 1960. It had become something of a tourist attraction. So many people were stopping to look at it and walk on the bridge that it, along with the other old crossings, became a footnote back in time.

Bridge to Watkins School.

Collings bridge, looking south, upstream. Oscar Freeman Collings is on the bridge.
His brother Zebulon is the tall man.

Byrne bridge near the author's home on Palmer Creek, 1933. L-R: Maud Byrne Watson, Mamie Foley, Bernard Watson, Florence McKee, Gladys Byrne, Patrick Foley.

Cary Culy's swinging footbridge near Kinney Creek.

Covered Bridges

As a young girl, I used to travel through the covered bridge at Applegate and two other covered bridges, Cameron and McKee, in the Upper Applegate. To enter a covered bridge in the summer was a refreshing escape from the penetrating sun, with an offering of a cool breeze inside. In winter a covered bridge also was a good place to escape from the rain or snow. School children must have enjoyed walking through the bridges to school, as I once did with my school chums. They offered a place to run a race, without stepping on any of the cracks, or to holler as loud as one could, letting the sound bounce off the walls. They also could be places to just listen to the river gently flowing beneath.

Covered bridges were never built for future generations. A bridge's life span was not much over 35 years. Who would have thought, back then, a covered bridge would someday become a historic entity? If the Applegate covered bridge were here today, it would almost be a shrine in the valley, and the Applegate Historic Society would be truly blessed in having such a nearby treasure and attraction.

To be realistic, there is no way that the Applegate covered bridge could have been saved. When steel began to take the place of wood, bridge-building changed dramatically. The holding weight and longevity of steel were a tremendous improvement, and there was no longer a need to cover the bridges from the elements.

Like most covered bridges, our three were very dark inside. Accidents could occur when one entered the dark chambers from the bright sunlight or during the dark winter. The McKee Bridge had some window openings added in the 1940s after a car and truck had collided inside. The openings also allowed the air to circulate, which helped prevent deterioration.

Some covered bridges have been saved from destruction, nostalgia taking precedence over practicality, with money being donated to save and restore them.

Even though the Applegate covered bridge is no longer here, it will always be a cherished memory for those of us who used it and are left to tell something about it.

The first spanned bridge at Applegate was built around 1872 by Thomas Mee. (He also constructed the first bridge, called the Centennial, across the Rogue River, located at Rock Point, in 1876. Thomas and his brother, James, were farmers and loggers living on Thompson Creek.)

In 1892, Jackson County built the covered bridge on the Applegate, which saw many years of service by the increasing population of farm people living here. Forty-two years later the bridge was in need of repair, and Jackson County opted for a replacement. Some time in February 1934, the new 180-foot span of steel was started, to be finished in June. The Mountain States Construction company of Eugene did the construction, with Fred Lindsay as superintendent. The cost was $32,806.

The Applegate Valley began preparing a celebration for the dedication of their new bridge. A committee investigated the cost of a bronze plaque bearing the "Pioneer Bridge" name. The state highway commission agreed to install the plaque for free.

The sponsors of the event were the Applegate Community League, Applegate Grange, and the Applegate Extension Unit. They invited all southern Oregon and northern California residents but made a special effort to invite all the pioneers of the region to participate. A picnic lunch would be at noon. Those participating were asked to bring their own eatables and table service. Coffee would be free, and the Home Economics Club of the grange would have cold drinks and ice cream for sale.

The celebration brought together one of the greatest turnouts of "old settlers" ever seen in the vicinity. Mrs. Louisa (Zelmore) Ray, 87, cut the ribbon, symbolizing the formal opening of the fine new span for traffic. She had come West in 1851 and was married (her second time) in Jacksonville nineteen years later, in 1872. She was the only surviving Granger of the 1870s and had been a resident of the Applegate longer than any other woman.

Aubrey Edwards was master of ceremonies. The program started at 2 pm with an invocation, followed by community singing with a Grants Pass band accompaniment, then an address by C.E. Gates of Medford. The band played again. Then Arthur S. Taylor, of Southern Oregon Normal School, in Ashland, gave an address. Pioneers were introduced, and the audience sang the Oregon State song with band accompaniment. The day's festivities ended with the ribbon-cutting and a big dance at the Applegate Hall that evening. Proceeds from the dance helped pay for the bridge's bronze plaque. (It can now be seen when entering the bridge from the north.)

I am very grateful to Marguerite Black (now deceased) for sharing her copies of Maude Pool's "Big Applegate" newspaper articles, which appeared for many years in the *Medford Mail Tribune*. This valuable information enabled me to put this history together.

1915 field meet at the Applegate covered bridge.
Southern Oregon Historical Society 2756.

The family of Thomas and Drucilla (Wooldridge) Mee.

Applegate Farming and Ranching

To survive in the Applegate in the early days, one had to be a miner, a farmer, or a rancher. Farmers raised crops, and ranchers raised animals, mostly cattle, but what did you call them if they did both? Most Applegate landowners did both in order to feed their families and bring in an income. Some of the smaller pieces of land may have been "squirrel ranches," but, oddly, no one claimed to raise squirrels.

Both my grandfathers were gold miners until they eventually bought some Applegate farmland. My Byrne grandfather, who came from Ireland at age 19, spent much of his life mining at the large gold mines in Nevada. Some time in 1885 he came to Oregon and mined on Humbug and Forest creeks, where he owned and worked several claims. About five years later, on a trip into Jacksonville, he met a man in a saloon who was looking to buy some mining claims. Grandfather Byrne traded that man his mining claims for 160 acres of land, including a log house, located along the lower part of Squaw Creek.

This was the first home my grandparents had ever owned and marked the first time they would be making a living by farming. Their two sons, Carroll, 20, and John (my father), 13, were a great help in preparing the ground along the creek for a crop of potatoes. The family grew hay on the less fertile land for feeding the livestock—cattle, hogs, sheep, and chickens.

Unfortunately, my grandfather died in 1904, and Carroll died in 1912 in a Jacksonville quarry mine explosion. My father was left to run the farm until the economy of the country forced him and his family to move. This land is now mostly under the Applegate Lake.

My McKee grandfather bought 160 acres near Palmer Creek in 1908 after he had "struck it rich" in a gold mine at the headwaters of Palmer Creek. A large nugget made the down payment on the farm, which had the Applegate River running through it. Even with the Applegate River as part of the ranch, water for irrigation came from two other streams. The east side of the land was irrigated with a ditch line coming from Beaver Creek, and the west side used Palmer Creek. The watering system could take up a lot of the farmer's time, as maintenance was a constant job. In the spring, after the high-water flows, the ditches would be cleaned and the intake repaired if damaged by flooding. All through the year, repairs were ongoing, whether from the drafted gophers making lots of holes or from washouts from too heavy a rainfall. Many of these water ditches are still in evidence or even in use to this day in the greater Applegate area.

Grandfather worked the fields with a team of horses, taking several weeks to do both sides of the ranch. The seeding was done by hand, with red Mexican beans on the east side and hay on the west side. My mother told how the dry beans were loaded into a horse-drawn wagon in the fall and taken to Jacksonville to sell. She and her two brothers had to make the 18-mile trip with their father, jumping up and down on the beans to free them from their shells.

When the Blue Ledge Copper Mine opened in 1906, farmers and ranchers had a handy market for their produce. The mine's voucher records from 1906 through 1916 show names of some Applegate farmers and ranchers: George Culy sold some apples for $21; Pat Swayne, apples for $20; John Offenbacker, potatoes for $60; William Lowden, hay for $263.92. Other names in the voucher listed the commodity but not the money value: Miles Cantrell, potatoes; M.A. Watkin, meat; John Byrne and Carroll Byrne, potatoes, mutton, hogs, hay; G.C. Culy, cattle and hogs; Mrs. R.J. Cameron, vegetables; R. Phillips, beef; C.M. Ruch Store, eggs and butter; Bert Harr, hay and potatoes; Amos McKee, apples, beans and vegetables; Mrs. M.I. Ray, turkeys; A.D. McKee, beef, hay, and feed. Even E. Britt from Jacksonville is shown to have sold honey to the company.

Cattle became the main source of income for most farmers in the Upper Applegate. In spring, after branding cattle with an identifying mark, ranchers would drive them into the higher mountains to feed on the lush grasses of the mountain meadows. The drive, on foot or by horseback, could take the rancher several days, so many had cabins in the high country to stay in before heading back. (Few of these still exist. The Krouse Cabin, on Grayback Mountain, burned a few years ago.) The rancher would then plant and harvest grass or alfalfa hay on the lowland ground. As the snow began to fly in the mountains, the cows would head down to these low pastures and feed on the harvested hay.

Weather conditions could wipe out a farmer's crop, be it vegetable, fruit, or hay. Sometimes the early cutting of hay in June would be ruined by a rainstorm. The next crop usually made it in our hot, dry summers, and, if lucky, a farmer could harvest a third crop in the fall. After the hay was cut and "cured for a few days," it would be raked and made into shocks, which were loaded onto a wagon and hauled to a barn to keep dry. It took at least three people to make this process work efficiently: one to pitch the shocks onto the wagon; a driver, who also had to stack the hay evenly; and someone at the barn to run the derrick horse. Using a rope with a large hay fork on one end for grabbing the hay, this horse pulled the hay to an opening in the upper part of the barn. The person standing in that opening would give a yell when the horse needed to stop and would then release the fork, dropping the hay into the storage area of the barn. My sister and I often did the derrick horse part, being very attentive to do it right.

[Editor's note, by Laura Ahearn: Evelyn's notes of a 1981 interview with her mother, Pearl, say that Amos "sold the mine (i.e., his partnership interest in the Ray Mine) in 1908 and purchased a farm." The deed conveying the farm from Manuel and Margaret Silva to Amos and Lottie is dated May 5, 1908—but they took possession as renters at least a year earlier (or as early as 1906), given that Maryum McKee was living there for well over a year prior to her death on October 22, 1908. The McKees purchased the farm with $2,500 borrowed from Zachary Cameron. A warranty deed and bond were recorded immediately after the Silva deed, requiring payment at eight percent interest over three years. We can't say how the gold nugget played into this real estate transaction.]

Harr ranch: Grandpa Beaver and John Harr, on the Bert Harr Ranch.
Upper Applegate, hoeing strawberry plants.

Amos McKee ranch: A river runs through it, as in the Applegate.
Looking south, one sees the Red Buttes Wilderness area.

Branding: Ernest Dorn, with branding iron; John Byrne, squatting; Bert McKee on horse at right; others unknown. John Byrne ranch on Squaw Creek around 1916.

Loading hay at the Collings Ranch at Watkins.

Ruffled Feathers

Turkeys! Not my favorite farm animal. Actually, I can't remember seeing very many turkeys on Applegate farms, but my McKee grandmother had half a dozen or so. She always fixed a turkey dinner for Thanksgiving and Christmas, and I did not mind their demise for a good reason. To a young child they seemed so big and frightening, and, since they were not fenced in, they roamed wherever I might be.

I did not mind crossing the scary footbridge over the river and making the quarter-mile walk to grandmother's, but escaping those turkeys before getting to her front gate was quite a challenge. Those turkeys would chase me, probably thinking I had some food. On one of my visits I stayed until Grandmother said it was beginning to get dark and I better get home. I took off in a hurry, and on the way I walked under some big fir and pine trees. Then I felt some splats on my head. I looked up and saw those darn turkeys roosting on the limbs above. I was so mad!

Years later my brother raised the same kind of turkeys on his ranch here in the Upper Applegate. He started with a small flock and found them quite profitable. He kept the hens, selling the eggs to a hatchery. I helped with some of the egg gathering. One old hen did not like my taking her eggs. When I made the gathering, about every hour, she would bristle up and give me a good peck on my hand. My brother said to throw her over the fence into another area, since she wanted to sit on her eggs and become a momma. So I then tried to get a hold of her tail feathers before she could peck me, but she would spring from her nest and outrun me.

I became exhausted after each chase around that big nesting area. Finally I managed to grab a part of her tail, which left her with fewer feathers. Eventually, she lost all of them, and I still was unable to catch her. That's when my brother couldn't stop laughing at my problem and came to help. He soon took care of it by outrunning her. She would still ruffle her feathers and bristle whenever she saw me coming near. Poor thing—she did look funny with no tail feathers.

In the spring my brother's large brooder house would be full of young ones that were later turned out in his fields to finish growing on a special mix of grains put in feed boxes. In following years, the boxes were replaced with large metal self-feeding containers, which saved time and energy in keeping the turkeys fed. My brother soon found the turkeys were more profitable than his cattle and began raising large flocks of the white, broad-breasted ones, both for eggs and meat. A truck would come to take the turkeys for processing before Thanksgiving and Christmas.

For many years the turkey ranch on Upper Applegate Road, and even a second ranch on Highway 238 in Ruch, were landmarks well known by locals. Eventually progress put my brother out of business as it became cheaper to have large operations all in one big building.

Years went by without seeing a turkey in the Applegate, but now I see the same old kind of turkeys that my grandmother and brother first had. I don't know if there really were wild turkeys here in those days. I don't remember ever seeing any. All I can say is that I don't dislike them now, but when they come in my yard, I sure get tired of chasing them. Again!!

[Editors' note: Wild turkeys are not native to Oregon. The birds were introduced beginning in 1961 to benefit game hunters. The Rio Grande strain that thrives in southwest Oregon was brought from Texas in 1975.]

Morris Byrne and his large flock of turkeys on Upper Applegate Road circa 1942.

Early Post Offices

I remember how, during the 1930s, my sister, Gladys, and I looked forward to "mail day," when a letter or package from a mail order company was expected. We would cross over the river on our wire footbridge to the main road, where our mailbox was. Then we would sit and anxiously wait for the arrival of the stage. It seemed like hours before we heard it coming up the old dusty road. I think there were three deliveries a week—on Monday, Wednesday, and Friday.

In those days the stage also carried passengers. Many people were without transportation and sometimes depended on this service. You could also leave a note in the mailbox with some money for stamps, maybe a list for a few groceries or a desperately needed item from the drug store. Those things would be delivered at no charge on the next mail day. A good relationship with the mail carrier went a long way to ensure you got this added service.

Before the rural free delivery came into being in the early 1900s, people relied on small post offices set up in a supply store, a barn, a room in someone's home, or maybe even a vacant building. Some of these post offices seemed way off the beaten path, but the luxury of this form of communication was very important to the farmers and miners living in the Applegate area.

My grandmother, Katie Byrne, became the postmaster of the Watkins Post Office in 1910, while it was in a storage shed near her house on Squaw Creek. This post office started in 1893 in the woodshed of Mark Watkins, whose son Anthony had been carrying the mail once a week from Herling (later Bauten), about four miles west of Jacksonville, to his neighbors in the upper Applegate. After seven years, Ed Faucett assumed the duties and moved the post office to his home. The Ed Langley ranch became the next home of the post office, and then Albert Collings became postmaster in 1904. The name Collings may be familiar with many of you, as there is a Collings Mountain near Applegate Lake.

Having a post office and getting the mail to your area were not always easy. Just looking at the snow in pictures of the Byrne Ranch and Watkins Post Office (now under Applegate Lake) shows how weather played a big part in how often you got mail. Many times the fords on the Applegate River were flooded or the trail washed out. Not until the Cameron and McKee covered bridges were built, in 1917, did mail delivery become reliable in the upper Applegate area.

The Watkins Post Office finally closed in 1920, after moving from the Byrne ranch to the Harr ranch father up Squaw Creek. Mrs. Louise Harr and then her daughter Grace were the last postmasters to stamp the Watkins, Oregon, postmark on outgoing mail.

The first post office for lower Applegate began in 1858. John O'Brien applied for the position of postmaster, but records show that John McKay took the position. Next were George Keeler in 1860, William Fowler in 1861, James Wilson in 1863, and Kasper Kubli in 1868. Kasper ran a store, so the post office was most likely in the store. Rial Benedict was next, in 1871, John H. Luman in 1874, John Pearson and John Bolt in 1875, Henry Kubli in 1887, and Orlando Rose in 1895. John Pernoll, who also ran a store at Applegate, was postmaster in 1900 and Laura Pernoll in 1938. The Applegate Post

Office was until recently a substation of Jacksonville's post office. For 148 years someone had made sure the community had a place to receive and send mail.

The Southern Oregon Historical Society has more information about the many post offices that sprang up in our area like Uniontown, Sterlingville, Buncom, Steamboat, Elliott Creek, Copper, Ruch, all reflecting the little nooks and crannies that make up the wonderful place we call the Applegate.

[Editors' note: The Southern Oregon Historical Society can be found at sohs.org.]

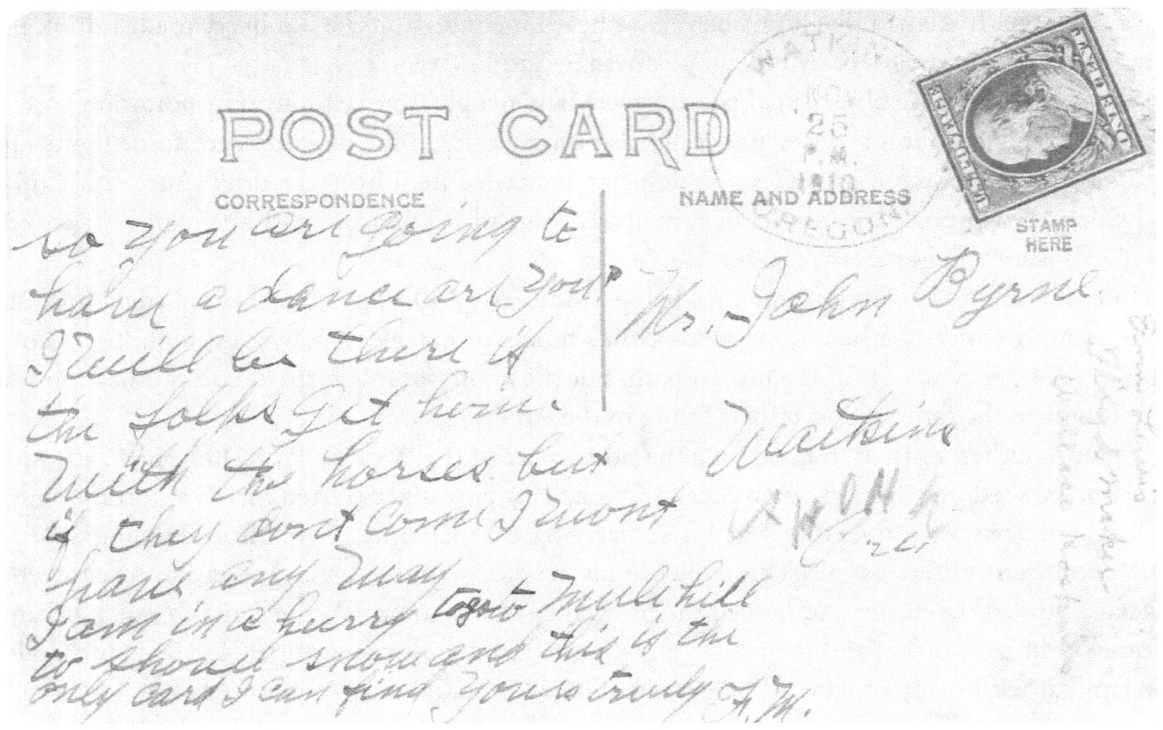

1910 postcard to John Byrne from Evelyn's uncle, Floyd McKee, delivered by Grandma Katie Byrne, the postmaster of Watkins.

Maude and Grace Harr and Katie Byrne Jr. at the Watkins Post Office around 1913.
A buggy has just brought the mail.

My Father at Applegate School

The first Applegate School was built in 1879-1880 on land donated by Rial Benedict. This school was on the west side of Humbug Creek near where the surviving Applegate School stands today.

My grandparents were living on Humbug Creek, where my dad, John Byrne, was born in 1887. His oldest sister and brother were already going to Applegate School. The family moved from there to Forest Creek and then to Watkins in the Upper Applegate area. However, an Applegate School card lists my dad in attendance while he was staying with the family's good friends, the John O'Briens, who lived a few miles from the school.

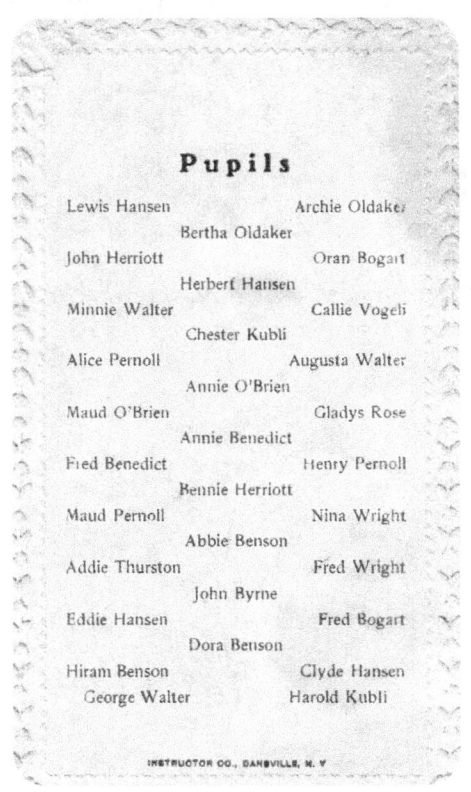

Pupils

Lewis Hansen	Archie Oldaker
Bertha Oldaker	
John Herriott	Oran Bogart
Herbert Hansen	
Minnie Walter	Callie Vogeli
Chester Kubli	
Alice Pernoll	Augusta Walter
Annie O'Brien	
Maud O'Brien	Gladys Rose
Annie Benedict	
Fred Benedict	Henry Pernoll
Bennie Herriott	
Maud Pernoll	Nina Wright
Abbie Benson	
Addie Thurston	Fred Wright
John Byrne	
Eddie Hansen	Fred Bogart
Dora Benson	
Hiram Benson	Clyde Hansen
George Walter	Harold Kubli

INSTRUCTOR CO., DANSVILLE, N. Y.

Applegate School, 1902   SOHS Photo #153?

1899 photo of young John and tall William Carroll Byrne with the O'Brien family (l-r): John, Mary Maude, Anna, Sarah, Rose, and Robert Emmett, who would marry Stella Byrne a year later.

Watkins School, Now under Water

Some of Applegate Valley's early one-room schools were made from logs harvested from a nearby forest. The Watkins School, built on a bluff high above the Applegate River, close to the road, was one such school.

The children played games of baseball, races, marbles, and touch tag in the roadway, as the teacher was always worried about a pupil falling off the cliff behind the school. Seldom did a vehicle pass by on the road, but when a copper ore wagon from the Blue Ledge Mine went by, play would stop for an exchange of greetings, especially if the children knew the driver.

Our family was quite involved with this school. Aunt Katie, my dad's youngest sister, attended the latter grades, and her older sister, my Aunt Margaret, taught there. When my brother, Morris, was six, in 1922, he attended first grade there. His teacher was Ina Stokes (later Pursel), a dear friend who boarded at my family's house during the school year.

This photo is of special interest because of the flag flying above the doorway. There does not appear to be a pulley system, so the flag must have stayed up during the entire school year, and some brave soul had to climb a ladder to remove the flag at the end of the school season.

A new school was later built on the Bert Harr property to accommodate the growing population, and the logs from the old school were hauled several miles down the road by Cary Culy to build a garage. So many years have gone by, and the old Watkins School is now only a memory beneath Applegate Lake.

Watkins School was built on a bluff above the Applegate River,
but is now under Applegate Lake.

Beaver Creek School District, 1898

As I wrote in an earlier article ("First Year at Beaver Creek School"), I attended first grade at Beaver Creek School, but the first school building in the Beaver Creek School District was the McKee School, on the other side of the river, that my mother and her brothers sometimes attended.

By 1898 the census indicated that about 35 eligible students between the ages of four and 20 lived in what is now the McKee Bridge area. Beaver Creek School District 82 was organized that year, and a building was constructed on government land that would become part of Deb McKee's property. (Deb was an older brother of my grandfather, Amos.) The builders, Charles Pursel and Oliver Dews, used rough lumber from the Pursel Mill for the board-and-batten construction. The building had windows on two sides, and my mother thought a roofed porch was added later. There are no pictures of the entire building, just a photo with students standing along one wall.

The first teacher, in 1898-99, was Miss Daisy Walker. Later, in 1899, Miss Kate Buckley, of Ruch, taught at the school. Her salary was $30 per month. The school year consisted of two three-month terms: spring (March, April, and May) and fall (September, October, and November). In summer, school was closed because most of the boys and girls had farm work to do, and in the winter, the weather was harsh enough to keep people home. Many times the boys would be young men by the time they graduated because they attended school only when they had time off from their chores. Girls sometimes didn't worry about graduating because they would be helping with their siblings or even starting their own families while only in their teens, such as my mother did.

The school clerk took a census every year, and county school funds were paid based on the number of pupils in each district. The 1898-99 count had family names like Lewis, Sargent, Pursel, Thomason, Silva, Carter, Dews, Buck, Creed, Bendick, and Kleinhammer.

There were fourteen students for the September 4 through November 25, 1899, school term—quite a large class considering the transportation mode of the students. They walked or rode horses, and, if a student lived on the opposite side of the river from the school, that student would most likely ride in the trolley.

The trolley was a wooden box suspended above the river by large cables from big trees or the highest rock outcrops. Students pulled themselves across with a pull rope. Then the students waiting to cross next would pull the empty trolley back so they could get in the box and, of course, pull themselves over the river. One photo shows teacher Ina Rozeltha Stoker pulling a trolley to her near what was the Nick Wright crossing. Another photo shows Orpha Lewis, Aletha Buck, and teacher Maude Harr on their way across the Applegate River near the school and what is now the cement McKee Bridge.

In 1903 my great-uncle, Deb McKee, settled on a mining claim on the east side of the river. His children began going to the school with my mother, Pearl McKee, and her brothers, Floyd and Earnest. That the land the school was situated on belonged to the McKees and that a large number of McKee children went to the school are the most likely reasons the school building became known as the McKee School.

[Editors' note: Some of this historical information was gathered from John and Marguerite Black's book, Ruch and the Upper Applegate Valley, *originally published in 1989.]*

Trolley from the McKee home to the Palmer Creek school, 1909.
L-R in the box: Orpha Lewis, Aletha Buck, and teacher Maude Harr.

Trolley across the river. Ina Rozeltha Stoker, Beaver Creek school teacher, 1906-07.

Schoolchildren at McKee School 1909. Front row, left to right: Luella McKee, Doris McKee, Fern Phillips, Ora Phillips, Vernie Stephenson, Homer Stephenson, Leonard McKee.
Middle row: Aletha Buck, Orpha Lewis, Lydia Lewis, Harold Bostwick.
Back row: Floyd McKee, Henry Bostwick, Fort McKee, Clarence Buck, teacher Maude Harr.

Logtown Cemetery Comes Alive!

Several years ago, after Carl Offenbacher made and donated a beautiful wrought-iron gate to Logtown Cemetery, the Logtown Cemetery Association made plans to remove the old falling-down fence and install new fencing to go with the gate. Even with some monetary donations and willing volunteers to do some of the work, the project seemed beyond the financial capabilities of the Logtown Cemetery Association. As time went on and more ideas were sifted through, a solution began to evolve that has brought the old cemetery its new look: a black chain link fence that runs along the front and a no-climb field fence enclosing the three other sides.

I would like to thank all the wonderful volunteers who worked on removing trees, brush, and old fencing. Though I have been asked not to list their names, as they seem to be shy about their good deeds, I feel blessed to live in a community with them in it. I would also like to thank the entities that helped the association secure the necessary capital to buy and install the fence: Oregon Parks and Recreation Division (with an Oregon Historic Cemetery Grant), Oregon Community Foundation (with a gift from Maggie Purves), McKee Bridge Historical Society, and the Logtown Cemetery Association (for keeping the project on the front burner).

Some of the following history of the cemetery is from John and Marguerite Black, who were charter members of the cemetery association. For many years Marguerite was the secretary, and John was the sexton. They are now buried in the cemetery that they loved so much and to which they donated their valuable time.

On September 20, 1892, John M. McKee sold his 160-acre homestead at Logtown to Austin Albright for $600. This included a two-story log house, barns, sheds, farmland, and some mining ground. It also included the graveyard, which by this time contained several rows of graves of miners and early settlers, some of them McKees. However, McKee's deed to Albright did not mention any land set aside or reserved for a cemetery. Legal ownership of this graveyard was passed along to each purchaser of the property until 1929.

The old cemetery, then called Laurel Grove, was located about 400 feet up the hill on the east side of the Jacksonville-Crescent City Road (now Highway 238). In 1929, a group of local people rebuilt the wire fence with new cedar posts donated by Mark Winningham. No written records of burials were kept in the early days, but Elva Smith, who grew up near Logtown and knew everyone, kept track of names and dates on hand-drawn maps as best she could during the 1920s and 1930s. Ike Coffman, long-time sexton of the Jacksonville Cemetery, often assisted with burials in Logtown during the 1930s.

The Logtown Cemetery Association was formally organized at a meeting held at the cemetery on May 14, 1939. Those who attended were Elva and Ed Smith, Pearl and Harry Whitney, Bill and Gertrude Winningham, L. Frank and Anna Lozier, Emma Smith, E. Igo and wife, Minus and Osie Pence, Leonard McKee, and John and Marguerite Black. They voted to change the name of the cemetery back to Logtown and agreed that all persons who had relatives buried there or owned a plot were considered members with a right to attend annual meetings and vote.

In a subsequent meeting, the association filed applications for incorporation and made plans to obtain legal title to the south half of the cemetery. Property owners of portions of the cemetery were Walter W. and Edith Bell, residing in California, and Paul E. and Mildred Pearce, residing in the Applegate. Both parties graciously donated land to the association.

The cemetery has gone through a few facelifts over the years. In 1939 a rustic archway with a carved wooden sign, donated by the local Civilian Conservation Corps, was installed. In 1949 the cedar archway became unsafe and was replaced with railroad iron and a wire gate. A well was drilled in 1950 and a hand pump installed. In 1958 a group of members planted a row of slips from Maryum McKee's yellow rose bush (Logtown rose) along the front on the north side of the gate. Later, the Applegate Garden Club set out more slips on the south side of the gate.

There are only a few of us old-timers left with memories and stories of the people buried there There are probably more McKees or relatives of the McKees buried there than other families, but there is no doubt that a who's who of the Applegate is etched in stone throughout the cemetery.

Construction of the cedar arch and cattle guard in 1939.
Bill Winningham, Ed Smith, and Walter Armpriest dig the trench, watched by (we believe)
Pearl (Winningham) Whitney and Letha Jean (Walker) Whitney. Photo source: Annice O. Black collection.

The wrought-iron gate was made by Carl Offenbacher,
who donated and dedicated the gate in 2008.

Baseball in the Applegate

Baseball was once one of the most entertaining activities here in the Applegate. How the boys and young men found time to practice the game while mining or farming is amazing, but play they did.

Several teams were organized throughout the region as early as 1910. My father, John Byrne, wrote a poem about a game between the Watkins Cubs and a team from Jacksonville. Watkins was an area, now under the Applegate Lake, named after the Mark Watkins family, some of the first settlers in the Upper Applegate. The poem names Fort McKee, Floyd McKee, Ramey Phillips, Wallace and Oren Haskins, Francis Collings, Frank Edwards, Gene (?), and Robert Watkins as players. It also mentions losing the game, with the players having every intention of evening the score next time.

The Watkins Cubs changed their name in 1911 or 1912 to the Palmer Creek Baseball Team. This team had a box social and dance event at Amos McKee's place on April 28 to raise money for team uniforms. Ladies brought box lunches to be auctioned off. Also, a new name was desired for the team, so the women who brought lunches wrote their suggestions on the outside of an envelope in which they had sealed their names. The winner would receive a one-dollar box of candy. Christine Harr's winning name was the Blue Jays or, as I sometimes heard, the Palmer Creek Blue Jays. Enough money was raised for the team to buy blue uniforms trimmed with white buttons and a wide belt.

Many times a baseball game was only part of the activities that people came from miles around to attend. In 1912 or 1913 the 4th of July was celebrated at Swayne Flat* with a Blue Jays baseball game, a literary and musical program, short foot races, and a 100-yard race with a purse prize of $5, as well as sack races, three-legged races, bicycle races for boys under 20, and untrained saddle horse, pony, trotting horse, and mule races. A whopping $10 prize was given to the winners of a tug of war.

Even the baseball games were a serious affair with $20 going to the winning teams. That day the scores were Blue Jays 12, C.J.s 7, Applegate 9, Jacksonville 7. To cap off the day's event there would be a Grand Ball. Many times a platform would be built for the dance, which would go on until the wee hours of the morning.

As a young child my first introduction to a baseball game was at Nick Wright Flat.** This was a large bare area with a few trees near the baseball field. People would arrive early to select the shaded spots. I remember it being terribly hot and the older people taking folded newspapers to fan themselves.

Sometimes there were unfriendly arguments about the umpire's call, and to me it seemed like the umpire was in great danger. I did not understand the booing and name calling, nor that it was considered part of the game. However, I soon learned that I was not above doing this, too, whenever a call went against a member of my family. My father usually played second base, my uncle Floyd McKee pitcher, and my brother, Morris, wherever he was needed. Often they would be on opposing teams, making it very hard to decide whom to root for.

In later years baseball was still a favorite pastime for me. I remember listening with my father to the World Series on our old battery radio. We were always for the underdog, the Brooklyn Dodgers. How we disliked those New York Yankees because they almost always won!

[Editors' notes: *Swayne Flat: The property was first owned by John Wright, then by Theodoric Cameron, who sold it to Patrick Swayne in 1892. Miles Cantrall bought it in 1907. Several other owners had the land until 1930, when Fred Straube bought it (according to Ruch and Upper Applegate Valley, by John and Marguerite Black). The Straube family had a dairy farm there for many years. It is located on East Side Road in the Upper Applegate.

**Nick Wright Flat: Nicolas Wright was one of the earliest settlers in the Palmer Creek area. In the 1870-80s his ranch was a stopping place for miners and packers. He had a store with basic supplies and a post office. Nick Wright Flat is located on the east side of Upper Applegate Road, just before Mule Mountain. My brother, Morris Byrne, bought the land in the 1940s, raising cattle and turkeys until his death in 1996.]

The Watkins Cubs baseball team, circa 1909, back row (l to r) Frank Collings, Oscar Collings, Zeb Collings, Bill Anderson, Bob Watkins; front row (l to r) Homer Stephenson, John Byrne, Vernie Stephenson, Floyd McKee.

The Blue Jays baseball team, back row (l to r): Wallace Haskins, John Byrne, Bob Watkins, Floyd McKee, Oren Haskins, Homer Stephenson (bat boy); front row (l to r): Frank Edwards, Earl Bostwick, Fort McKee, Ramey Phillips, Ed Finley.

Applegate Grange

I recall the first time I went to the Applegate Grange Hall, probably at five years of age, with my parents, John and Pearl Byrne, for a dance. My parents and my maternal grandmother, "Lottie" McKee, had become members of this Grange. The hall seemed to be the biggest building I had ever been in. I was afraid to leave my mother's side. Then a little girl came to my rescue. She was Beverly Mee, my age, and ever so friendly.

We danced together and had a great time sliding up and down the slick dance floor when the music stopped. When refreshments were served at midnight, Beverly took me to meet her mother, Martha Mee, who was working in the kitchen with other Grange ladies. I also met Beverly's father, Tom, and her sister, Barbara. When they moved to Medford, I spent much time at their home, as Beverly and I went through Medford High School together.

The Grange held meetings in the large Community Hall, a board-and-batten building at the location of what is today the restaurant called the Applegate Country Club.

The following information came from *Ruch and the Upper Applegate Valley*, by John and Marguerite Black.

"The history of this hall goes back to the first World War. A so-called Socialist Party was organized in the area. This group raised money in the neighborhood and built a meeting hall. It was not a very successful organization, and they disbanded in the early 1920s. Three local men, Chester Kubli, Warren Mee, and Bert Clute, decided to buy the hall and donate it to the school district for meetings and programs. They organized a Community League, which raised money to help pay for the hall. All kinds of activities were held, dances being the most popular. Eventually the school board returned the ownership of the hall to the Community League. The League then gave it over to the Applegate Grange."

The Applegate Grange was organized September 27, 1930. There were forty-one charter members, among them my aunt, Clara O'Brien.

The Grange was very active from its beginning. One of the interesting projects in 1931 was the reseeding of poa bulbosa grass following a forest fire that destroyed parts of Humbug Creek and China Gulch. The grass was donated by Charley Hoover, a prominent Central Point farmer. Grange master Sid Hansen stacked his truck high with the sacks of seed and took them to the burned destination, where many Grangers helped sow the seed. I wonder if that grass has replenished itself and can be seen there today?

The Grange Hall became a busy community center. In her series for the *Medford Mail Tribune*, "Big Applegate News," Maude Pool records a number of events there. On March 9, 1934, Jacksonville High School presented a two-act operetta, featuring many Applegate students. Among them were Frank Mee, Henry Head, Gladys Byrne, June Peebler, June Provolt, Alice Madson, Eileen Berry, Lola Fields, Lois Matheny, Marion Roberts, Jack Provolt, and Bud Peebler.

The Rogue River Girl Scouts presented a play at the Grange Hall entitled "Ain't Women Wonderful" on February 14, 1935. They also did tap dancing, songs, stunts, and old-fashioned quadrilles. On April 13, 1935, the Applegate Home Extension Unit presented a one-act comedy entitled "Cabbages" at the

Applegate Grange Hall. On June 6, 1935, Maude Pool wrote, "Plans for elaborate observance of Labor Day are under way here by the local grange. A rodeo and barbecue will be held on Thompson Creek according to arrangements being made by the ways and means committee of which Frank Knutzen is chairman." The list goes on and on of bazaars, fairs, political speakers, almost always with a dance to follow. Unless, of course, the dance was the main event.

According to state Grange records, the Applegate Grange dissolved in 1955, when they surrendered their charter. Why such an active Grange of 25 years would dissolve was a mystery. Rumors abounded, one being that a proposal to build a new Grange hall divided the members, and attendance and membership dropped beyond recovery. From John and Marguerite Black's book: "By then the old building was so dilapidated it was falling apart so it was dismantled. In 1989 all that remains is a vacant lot overgrown with trees and bushes."

The Applegate Valley divides geographically into the Lower, Little, and Upper portions of the Applegate. Only the distance and mode of travel in the early days kept residents somewhat apart, as the socializing at dances, baseball games, picnics, and school functions kept friendships close. The Applegate Grange added to this and brought such people as my family from the Upper Applegate to its many educational and recreational events.

Memories abound for me whenever I pass the place where the Grange once stood. I can still hear the friendly voices, often with laughter, and the dance music. Grange meetings were somewhat boring for me then, but it is those kind faces I recall the most. My heart is filled with gratitude for having been with these wonderful people who were once the early settlers in the Applegate Valley. This community is still filled with good people, but the life has changed to a much faster pace. Socializing is not the "knock on the door, come on in, you're just in time for dinner or supper" bit. It now seems to require a phone call first, to make an appointment, and sometimes to enter through a locked gate. It is all part of modernization, along with cell phones, automobiles, televisions, computers, shopping centers, supermarkets, sports arenas, fast foods, and credit cards.

Don't get me wrong—I would not want to change the conveniences I am now enjoying. What I miss is the families, young and old, getting together to socialize as they once did in the Applegate Grange.

THE APPLEGATE GRANGE 1931
(GRASS RESEEDING PROJECT)

Annual Play Day at the Applegate Schools

Schoolteacher Ina Pursel started an annual Play Day at Ruch School in May of 1932. She invited all of the Applegate's district schools to participate. There was Little Applegate, Uniontown (about one-quarter mile upstream from the mouth of Little Applegate River), Sterling Creek, Forest Creek, Watkins, Thompson Creek, Applegate and, of course, my own school, Beaver Creek.

The first Play Day that I remember was in 1937. It was such a big deal, with more than 100 participating school children. There was a flag salute and community singing led by P.A. Matheny with Miss Lois Matheny as pianist. Also, the Ruch Ladies Sewing Circle had a display of quilts, and the men played a game of baseball between Upper and Lower Applegate districts. Umpire Ray Offenbacher was accused of having poor eyesight because his lower Applegate team won the game.

Each school did a little performance. Beaver Creek had its harmonica band. Uniontown and Ruch each put on a play. Little Applegate presented folk dancing, and Sterling staged a wrestling match. There was also Forest Creek's book drill, Watkins's piano number, Thompson Creek's crowning of the May Queen, and Applegate's Maypole dance.

And then the real competition began with races like potato, three-legged, hop-step-and jump, wheelbarrow, and shuttle relays. There were 25-, 50-, and 75-yard dashes, high jumps and standing jumps, baseball throwing and chinning. Every child could find something to be in.

The 1940 Play Day is the most memorable for me because it was my last year at Beaver Creek School. I managed to place third in the baseball throw, and then, much to my surprise, I was first in the 75-yard dash. That was probably because I often ran the mile to school when I was late. Other Beaver Creek School winners that year were sister and brother, Lucille and Charles Culy; Elsie Dietrick and brother Harry; and brothers Dean and Orden Phillips—a good showing for our little Beaver Creek.

In June that year, the eighth-grade pupils from the Applegate Valley Schools received their diplomas at commencement exercises in Ashland. My cousin Doug McKee, Walter Offenbacher, and I were the only ones from Beaver Creek. Elsie Dietrick, my best girlfriend, wasn't with us because she had moved to Ruch that year and graduated with Edward Hawkins, Oren Kruse, Wanda Little, Irene McDonlough, Jeanne Norris, Donald Waggener, and Lois Zuiderweg. Applegate graduates were Carolyn Benedict, Beulah Brock, Jeanne Brown, Raymond Corbin, Beverly Mee, and Bill Wright. From Thompson Creek were Alvy Kendall and Roberta Smith, and from Forest Creek, Audrey Meads.

[Editors' note: Some of this information came from the "Applegate News" column by Maude Pool that ran in the Medford Mail Tribune *years ago.]*

Ruch School, May 16, 1914, (l to r) Mrs. Nellie Collins (teacher), "Cap" Ruch (clerk), Miles Cantrall (director), Charles Hamilton (director), Horace Venable (director).

The old log Watkins school, 1926.

Applegate School, 1938. Back row (l to r) Silas Davis, Fritz Offenbacher, Georgia Benedict, Lorraine Rowden, Billie Boussum, Miss Thelma Stringer (teacher), Jack Richie, Charles Rolls, Eleanor Corbin, LaDonna Gibson. Front row (l to r) Beverly Surran, Davy Crenshaw, Dickie Franks, Gary Denzer, Barbara Rolls, Temple Rose, Jimmie Hammons, Richard Huggins, Leonard Corbin, Harriet Taylor, Betty Jean Studebaker.

Uniontown School, 1912, (l to r) (?) Wolf, Jessie Garrett, Mae Lawrence (teacher), Cora Goldsby, Ora Colby, (?) Wolf, Paul Jennings, Louis Jennings, Lloyd Cameron, Bert Goldsby.

Some Old Gas Stations

A few years ago I was asked if I remembered the old gas service station on top of Jacksonville Hill. For some reason, I do not. Lorna Erskin, a Forest Creek friend, told me about one there in the 1930s and that Mr. Ed Demer had a photo of it. Well, it did not take me long to contact him, and he kindly let me have a copy. He remembered it quite well because his grandparents lived across the road from it.

I also found that Maude Pool, the Applegate news correspondent for the *Medford Mail Tribune*, wrote in a March 12, 1930, article: "New Station Going in near Applegate. Seeing an opportunity to serve the tourists and vacationists who flock to the Applegate in the summertime, T. S. Cady is preparing to open a service station, with free picnic grounds near his home at the summit of Jacksonville hill. Construction of the station, which will be operated in connection with the Union Oil Company, is well underway, and Mr. Cady expects to be ready for business in a short time. The new concern, which will be named the Summit Station, will include a line of lunch goods, and the inviting picnic grounds among the pines at the rear of the building will make it a favorite with the autoists. Mr. Cady is assisted with the carpenter work by I. E. Clapp. Mr. Cady, who has lived here since coming from Idaho a year ago, says he thinks Southern Oregon a fine place, and he is interested in the future progress and development of this country."

Now my research began for some other old gas stations in our area. In looking through John and Marguerite Black's book, *Ruch and the Upper Applegate Valley*, I found that the Ruch store had a gas pump. In the 1890s Casper "Cap" Ruch built a blacksmith shop, which evolved into a general store and post office, in the area we now call Sunshine Plaza. About 1915 he expanded the store building and installed a gas pump in the front.

Then competition started in 1928 when his nearby neighbors, Chester and Martin McDonough, built the Sunnyside Gas Station, with a lube and oil change pit. They sold tires, tubes, and other automobile supplies, and customers had convenient restrooms on the lower level. They added a stock of groceries some years later.

There were gas pumps at the Copper Store, which was built in 1934 by Mr. and Mrs. Crow. Many people wondered how this business could survive in such a remote area. But it did. Many people just took a Sunday drive up the Applegate to stop and visit with the locals there and have a soda pop or a beer and buy things for a picnic. It would probably still be there if the Applegate Dam had not been built, but now that store location is at the bottom of the lake.

I was told there were gas pumps sometime in the early 1940s at the small building by the McKee Bridge. The station didn't last long, and the building was later used by the Upper Applegate Lions Club for their meetings. The Upper Applegate Store (now McKee Bridge Store) had some gas pumps later, but they were discontinued when store owner Willard Wilson stopped using them.

Also, there was a gas station built in 1947 at Applegate across the road from the Pernoll's store (now the Applegate Store and Gas Station). Owners were Edward Kubli and his son, Norman.

I have no idea how many more early-day gas pumps sprang up here and there in our area, but I did find an interesting photo of some in Jacksonville. There were two pumps on the sidewalk in front of the Masonic Lodge building on California Street, and a 1925 photo shows a gas station at the end of California and 5th Street built by Mr. W.A. Childers and his son-in-law Mr. Leonard McKee, my great-uncle.

Old gas pumps are now considered antiques and are interesting to see in collections. They bring back nostalgia of those bygone days when you could fill your tank for a few cents and get away from the farm for a day of relaxation.

Service station at the top of Jacksonville Hill, 1930s.

Gas pumps on California Street in Jacksonville.
Photo by Margaret LaPlante.

Gas station at California and 5th streets, Jacksonville, 1925.

Maude (Pool) Ziegler

Starting in 1926, Maude "Maudee" Pool wrote about Applegate Valley news, which appeared in the *Medford Mail Tribune* for many years. She also contributed articles to three other southern Oregon newspapers for 20 years before joining the staff at the Tribune around 1957. Some of her Applegate Valley news articles were published in the Portland newspapers and other West Coast publications.

She was born December 23, 1907, the only child of Benton and Ada (Cameron) Pool. She spent most of her life in the upper Applegate on East Side Road about two miles from the Cameron Bridge. This pioneer property was at one time a part of her grandfather William Cameron's ranch. She and her parents lived in a log house, which was always immaculate and charming. I remember feeling so comfortable when visiting there. Even then, I liked the old furniture and handmade rugs that graced the wooden floors. I was surprised when Maudee confided in me that she did not like old furniture or old buildings, such as theirs.

Maudee was a most compassionate and friendly person, always welcomed wherever she went, either for a visit or an interview. Not once did I ever hear an unkind word about her. Everyone trusted her to report events and happenings with accuracy and diplomacy. I remember her sense of humor, especially when she revealed some happening about herself. Her enlightened audiences heard her contagious giggle with each episode. Even though Maudee was nineteen years older than I, it made no difference to her as she accepted any age with the same special attention.

I was about eight years old when she organized a group of people for a hike up the Boaz Mountain near her home. This is a very interesting mountain. The story goes that a Mr. Boaz had a ferry in the 1850s at the mouth of the Little Applegate River, close to Preston Bridge, and ferried the Chinese miners across the river for fifty cents apiece. Because of the ferry, Mr. Boaz was called "Captain." (The place is now the Pool ranch.)* The only members of the hiking party I remember were my sister, Gladys; the Beaver Creek School teacher, Bertha Haskins; and her husband, Wallace. There may have been others whom I do not recall. We left early one morning with a lunch and some Band-Aids for the expected heel blisters from ill-fitting shoes, which were normal for those days. Mrs. Haskins was rather heavyset, so it was just a matter of time before she began to show signs of fatigue. Having come from a city in Illinois, she probably had not climbed a mountain before. We left her somewhere on the climb to rest and wait for our return. Her husband had been raised in the Applegate but had not climbed Boaz mountain, so being a good sport, she insisted he go on and not spoil the outing. Maudee was always in good shape, lithe and energetic. That day, I had a hard time keeping up with her and was very tired by the time we reached the top. I was even more tired by the time we returned home, but that day was one of my most memorable times with Maudee.

When Beaver Creek Sunday School first started in the mid 1930s, Maudee had a part in its organization. There was no church here in the Upper Applegate, so the next best thing was a Sunday School. The attendance was minimal, but the enthusiasm was high. The services were first held in the Beaver Creek School (across the road from the Forest Service's Jackson Park), then in the Upper Applegate Grange hall when it was built, near the McKee Bridge, in 1936-37. Mr. Randall, a traveling minister, came about once a month. The rest of the time Mrs. Christine Harr conducted the services. Her father was a minister, so she was well qualified for doing this.

During this time Mr. Randall was asked to have an Easter Sunrise Service in the new McKee Bridge Park, which the CCC boys had built. The congregation met down by the river in a large rock-walled cove with seats. Our singing voices sounded even better with the accompaniment of the river. It was a very memorable occasion. After the service we went to the Grange Hall where the Grange ladies served breakfast, which included the most tasty homemade buttermilk pancakes I have ever eaten.

Maudee married William H. Ziegler Jr, on March 23, 1944. He worked for the Rogue River National Forest at the Applegate Star Ranger Station. Their only child, Robert, was born in 1945. Maudee's father died in 1946 and her mother in 1953. I think the Zieglers then moved into Maudee's old log home. Shortly after that, she made a phone call to me, asking if I wanted a couple of her old rocking chairs. They had stored one in the barn for several years, and the other one was too fragile to use anymore. Of course, I accepted these chairs without any hesitation. The next day they were sitting in my home, where they still are today. She was so happy to get rid of them and I was so happy to be the recipient.

Soon afterward, she got her wish of "out with old and in with new" when the family moved into a small mobile home in front of her old home. She was as happy as a clam in her new surroundings. Housework now was a snap, which left more free time, she said. She continued to write in very cramped quarters, but this did not bother her. She eventually decided to have the old log home dismantled and advertised the very large logs for sale. I do not know how long before the building was gone, but Maudee continued to tend to the existing lawn and flowers as before. Prior to her husband's death, in 1979, their son, Robert, with his wife and two sons, moved to a home on the hill above her.

Maudee belonged to the Upper Applegate Extension Unit and the Ruch PTA. Many of her articles included news about these organizations, as well as about the Applegate and Upper Applegate Granges. A newspaper (*Medford Mail Tribune*) article about her, dated about 1961, says her most exciting moments of corresponding were those which came in reporting election returns from the Applegate area. She once reported returns on the Townsend Plan from the Hutton precinct over the California line. The report was broadcast over Los Angeles and Salt Lake City radio stations. She said she thoroughly enjoyed writing about people and events. This made for many wonderful contacts with people and for writing offers. Besides, news writing was one of the very finest ways of making pin money in the country, she said.

During the years of devoting my time to raising my family, I rarely saw Maudee. Sad to say, when we did meet, it was usually at a funeral. I was always amazed how she never seemed to change. That's how I still remember her, and especially the last time I saw her. She was walking on East Side Road on her way to the McKee Bridge store for lunch. My husband's parents had once lived on this road, so we would occasionally drive to their old place to see the changes. That day, I was surprised to see Maudee walking along with her usual stride. She also was surprised to see us. We had such a nice chat before saying good-bye. Little did I know I would not see her again, for soon afterward she died, on March 4,

1990. She left us with a valuable record of what went on in our Applegate Valley during her lifetime, but now only a few of us remember her and her news about us, back in time.

Notes on Historical Events, Applegate Ranger District. (As related by Ranger Lee Port, 1945.)

[Editors' note: The Townsend Plan was a proposal made in 1933 for the government to pay $200 monthly to every person over age 60, with the requirement that the money be spent quickly to help alleviate the Great Depression.]

Maudee and grandfather, William Cameron.

Albert Young, Jeanette Gore, and Maude hiked to the Tallowbox Mountain lookout in 1928.

A BARNYARD TRAGEDY

By MAUDE POOL

It wasn't a big fire, not many things were lost and not many heard of it. That is just what human folks think about it, but to a patient little bantam hen it meant more than that. She lost her life in the fire which damaged the woodshed at the Walter Armpriest home at Ruch last week. She was burned as she was setting under the building, hovering a few large eggs (someone had traded for her tiny ones) which would soon have made her a proud mother.

The blaze started from a tub in which a fire had been placed for smoking meat in a corner of the shed. The building was slightly damaged, and there was a small loss in meat, fruit, and wood. The building was owned by Mrs. Anna Ruch.

Maude's newspaper career started in 1924. This report appeared in The Jacksonville Miner *on January 22, 1932.*

The Pool home.

Applegate Dam

The recent removal of some local dams and the consideration for removal of others bring back memories about the pros and cons of the Applegate Dam. Many old-timers living near the Applegate River wished for years for a dam to ease the flooding of their lands. Still others strongly objected to such a dam, its location, and the changes it would bring to the river. Here are some interesting facts from my scrapbook.

As early as 1962, opposition to a dam on the river arose at local gatherings. Some of the older landowners were worried that they would lose their free water rights for irrigating their fields. Others were actually worried about losing their lands. A petition against the dam was circulated that stated: With irrigation the only source of payment, the project is not fair and equitable to water users. The farm production of the United States does not require 5,000 new acres in the Applegate Valley. (I assume this means acreage no longer subject to flooding.)

The loss of at least seven miles of fish spawning beds above the dam will do more destruction than will be gained by the plans for fish enhancement. The quick benefits, such as employment, merchandise sales, land sales, rentals for workers, are not good long-range economics for the Applegate Valley. The dam will spoil the Applegate as a family recreation stream.

The deep reservoir would be dangerous for small children, access would be limited and difficult, and many camps would be flooded out and could not be replaced because of the steep terrain. The reservoir would be subject to severe fluctuations, up to draw-downs of 122 feet.

And then there was the cost. In 1974 the Corps of Engineers estimated a cost of $50.2 million to build the dam. By the next year the estimate was up to $63 million.

In 1976 a newly formed "Save the Applegate" group presented an alternative program for flood control. According to a March 2, 1976, article in the *Medford Mail Tribune*, it included an intensive reforestation program of the whole Applegate watershed, revised forestry road-building practices, river channel cleaning, and purchase of necessary lower Applegate floodplain lands. The plan would reduce heavy rain runoff and riverbank overflow, maintain present irrigation rights, and provide increased recreational access to the river. The association was seeking to halt further funding of the Applegate Dam, for which land was being purchased by the Corps. President Ford's budget already included three million dollars for the project.

Jackson County Commissioners had been contacted about a vote on the dam proposal during November general elections. Even though Jackson County would be left with all of the continued cost (e.g., road maintenance), after the dam was in, Josephine County Commissioners were also contacted because a substantial portion of flood control benefits would occur in their county.

Both counties were opposed to having a public vote on the proposal. In April 1976, the Save the Applegate Valley Association spent almost a week in Washington, DC, to convince Congress to support the idea of a local opinion vote. The vote never materialized.

By October 1, 1977, the price tag for the Applegate Dam was roughly $89.4 million. The plans for the dam had been changed several times in the past several years. The plan now called for a 242-foot-high, 1,200-foot-long, rock-fill dam about one-half mile downstream from French Gulch. When the lake was full, it would hold 82,000 acre-feet of water, making the lake about five miles long with an eighteen-mile shoreline.

Long periods of interruptions by governmental and citizens' actions finally gave way, and the first phase of the dam started in 1977, even though the bulk of the money had not been approved by Congress or President Carter. The Corps went ahead anyway and started acquiring private land in the upper Applegate Valley, getting the approved funds by the groundbreaking date of June 18, 1978.

The ceremony took place near the project site on the Applegate River at milepost 15 on Upper Applegate Road. The Rogue Basin Flood Control and Water Resources Association, the Committee to Revitalize our Applegate River, and the Upper Applegate Grange sponsored the groundbreaking event.

The dam was completed in October 1980 for $96 million. By March 1981 the reservoir behind the dam was more than half full and ready for a dedication on May 27. There were 350 people at the formal dedication, including Oregon Governor Atiyeh, Oregon Senator Hatfield, and other dignitaries. The sun shone down on the gathering of the man-made lake, an historic event. Was it worth the cost and the destruction of the little communities of Watkins and Copper, now beneath the waters? Only time will really decide that question. Those who had been against the project may now agree that it is at least a beautiful lake when filled and the snow-capped Siskiyou Red Butte mountains behind add to its luster.

This closing is by Eric W. Allen Jr, editor of the *Medford Mail Tribune*, May 27, 1981: "The Applegate Valley, jewel of the Siskiyous, now gains a new gem in a lake that will serve the many purposes of man…and will become a part of the history of an area with a rich historic background."

[Editors' note: Articles from the Medford Mail Tribune *were used for timeline and cost estimates.]*

Applegate Lake. Photo courtesy of Jan Wilts.

Albert Collings and Albert Williams (Evelyn's father-in-law) at the Copper Store in 1947, before the construction of the Applegate Dam.

Logtown

Each spring some little yellow roses peak out from a spindly small bush, now 156 years old, located in a mediocre spot along Highway 238 between Jacksonville and Ruch, Oregon. The rose bush is the only evidence left of the village of Logtown, a flourishing settlement comprised of a store, hotel, livery stable, two meat markets, two blacksmith shops, three saloons, two Chinese stores, a schoolhouse, and a church. This was not only the center of a raucous gold-mining area but a stage stop for an important supply road from Crescent City, California, to Jacksonville, Oregon. Some very interesting stories have been handed down through the descendants of the miners who first scratched for gold along the banks of Forest Creek. But for now, this is the story of the Harrison rose, originally from England, which we now call the Logtown Rose.

It is not an outstandingly beautiful rose, supported on very thorny stems with tiny leaves. It survives because the deer can't stand it and the gophers don't stay long. The poor soil and lack of water don't seem to matter, either. Even an overdose of spray from the county roadside weed sprayer didn't entirely do it in, although it didn't look well for a few years. A tree planted behind the rose has roots now competing for water and nourishment. As though that is not enough, the dreaded star thistle showed up to add to the distress of the already constant vibration from traffic. If it survives all of this, I guess it may outlive most of us.

It is very special to me and my family because it was planted at Logtown by my great-grandmother, Maryum Bowen McKee. She had brought the little rose across the plains with her from Sullivan County, Missouri, to the Rogue Valley in 1853. My great-grandfather, John McKee, was a blacksmith who invented an improvement to a miner's pick, which he called a "strap-eye pick." This pick was in great demand. He built a large log house in Logtown for Maryum and their two little children. At the front gate to the yard the tenderly cared for yellow rose found its new home.

My great-grandmother had twelve more children through the years. One died shortly after birth, and a daughter, Martha Jane, died at age nine. She was buried behind their house next to the hillside. (Her remains were later moved to the Logtown Cemetery.) When the gold mining petered out, my great-grandparents moved to Little Butte Creek near Butte Falls. Many years later when one of their daughters and her husband purchased a new automobile, they took John and Maryum to see their old place. It was Maryum's first ride in a car. They were heartbroken when they saw their old log house mostly gone. Only part of the front portion remained standing. A range cow was looking out of one of the window openings. They had spent most of their lives there, and now to find Logtown almost completely gone was hard to bear. As they were leaving, Maryum glanced over to a broken-down gate, and there she saw her little rose bush. Tears filled her eyes as she pointed it out to her family. "Look, my little rose is still alive."

There are a lot of descendants of this McKee family, and they knew where the little rose was, but nothing was done to preserve it until the Jacksonville Garden club encircled it with some protective white posts during Oregon's Centennial year in 1959 and the Applegate Valley Garden Club planted 60 more Logtown roses across the front of the Logtown Cemetery. The Jacksonville Garden Club had a granite marker made for a dedication ceremony later that year for the little rose. The marker was unveiled by Miss Teri Lee Wolfe, a great-great-granddaughter of John McKee. Two of John McKee's remaining children also attended and were introduced. They were Mary Thelma Higinbotham and John B. McKee. (It has been 50 years since that ceremony. Hard to believe.)

Sad to say, sometime later an out-of-control car ran into the granite marker and destroyed it. Rocks were then placed around the rose. The Applegate Valley Garden Club continued its care of the rose and the cemetery roses. In 1983 a member of the club, Myrtle Krouse, made a new wooden marker for the Logtown rose. It was a beautiful hand-carved scene of Maryum watering her little rose. Another ceremony was held for the nice addition. Three of the McKee's remaining grandchildren were among the attendees: Clara Smith, Pearl Byrne, and Dorothy Hackert. The rose and location of the cabin are only a few feet off Highway 238, almost straight across what is known as Longanecker Road.

In 1878 John McKee filed for and was granted a 160-acre homestead adjacent to the land his cabin was on. The graveyard where early Logtown miners and settlers were buried was just inside the south boundary of this land. Since this was a government land grant, he became the first "legal" owner of the property. Over the years several owners of the land had legal ownership of the cemetery, and all allowed its continued use as a cemetery. In 1939 an association was formed to make improvements and facilitate the continued use of the cemetery. Landowners Paul E. and Mildred Pearce and Walter W. and Edith Bell donated two pieces of land that had been used since the 1850s as a cemetery into the keeping of the Logtown Cemetery Association on October 17, 1940.

To see the Logtown rose you need to stop at the cemetery or at the rose marker on Highway 238 in the spring. A beautiful gate to the Logtown Cemetery was made and donated by Carl Offenbacher in 2008 that has a rendition of the rose on it. Or you can visit the Ruch Library where an outstanding wall mural by Marvin and Lilli Ann Rosenberg graces the lobby and has the yellow rose in it.

[Editors' note: Some information from Ruch and the Upper Applegate Valley, *by John and Marguerite Black.]*

*The youngest of John and Maryum's fourteen children, John B. (1878-1972) and
Mary Ithena (1876-1975), attend the dedication of the Logtown Rose plaque in the 1960s.*

Maryum Bowen McKee.

*Logtown marker with Clara McKee Smith, Pearl McKee Byrne,
and Dorothy McKee Hackert.*

Joseph and Almira McKee

Buried at Logtown Cemetery, Joseph McKee was an early settler in southern Oregon. Along with his wife, Almira, and their children, Joseph arrived in the Applegate in 1860 among a second wave of McKees. His son, John M. McKee, and family had already arrived in 1853. Joseph was receiving a pension from Frederick County, Virginia, for his service in the war of 1812. He was born in 1793 and died on April 19, 1870. Also buried at Logtown is Almira McKee, who was born around 1809 and died in 1882.

Joseph McKee

Almira McKee

Story of an Old Tintype

It doesn't take much to get sidetracked with my collection of old photos and the lack of information about them. There is one old tintype of the Eagle Hotel, built in Eagle Point by Arthur Pool in the mid 1870s. A dear friend, Vieva Saltmarsh, who lived up Little Applegate years ago, had a tintype and other old photos for me to make copies of. I asked Vieva why it was among her family photos, and she said her husband, Glenn, was related to the Pools.

At that time I didn't continue with the research, but much later I found more information in Gaynell Krambeal's 1979 book about Eagle Point. He said the hotel was built by Arthur Pool, who was born on January 8, 1834, in Bedford County, Pennsylvania. Arthur was a blacksmith by trade, but soon after his arrival in southern Oregon, he opened the Eagle Hotel, which became a regular stop on the railroad between Portland and San Francisco.

A book by Barbara Hegne, *Unforgettable Pioneers*, tells about Arthur and a neighbor. "At an earlier time in 1875, Arthur Pool and William Sutherland* engaged in what the newspaper termed 'an amazing bloodless encounter.' These two families resided on Butte Creek, and their children had the usual 'your kids are beating up my kids' syndrome. The two fathers became involved in a typical over-the-fence argument, carried over from the children. The two fathers began shouting at each other, and when that didn't work, they started pitching stones back and forth. Arthur Pool had the best advantage, being on the outside of Sutherland's yard. He used stones Sutherland had earlier thrown out of his yard to keep it clean. After several minutes of dodging rocks Sutherland saw he was definitely at a disadvantage. He rushed to his house, grabbed his pistol, and began shooting wildly at Pool. Arthur's blood ran cold when he saw how serious this was getting. He quickly hightailed it to notify the law. Sutherland was arrested and examined before Justice Tinkham. He was bound over in the sum of $200, which he furnished.'

Getting back to the Eagle Hotel tintype photo, it may be the only one now in existence showing the unfinished building. It shows children standing in the upper story opening and some boys sitting on the top of a lumber stack. Also, I find the slightly visible horse by the fence interesting. I think there must have been a double exposure of the tintype.

I find it so engaging how one photograph can lead to another photograph or story about our local history. And so I can bring us back to the Applegate, Little Applegate, to be exact, with the Saltmarshes.

Arthur Bird Pool had a daughter named Ella Clarinda. She married her third husband, Joseph Bolivar Saltmarsh, on November 24, 1881. Now, Joseph already had several children by his first wife, who died in 1878 and is buried in the Sterling Cemetery. One of these, a son named Arthur Bird Saltmarsh, married Ella's (the stepmother's) sister, Dora May Pool, on April 10, 1886. They had four children: Lee, Dean, Ossie, and Glenn. Arthur B. took up a homestead on the Little Applegate River near the mouth of Yale Creek. Glenn later farmed this land, where he and his wife, Vieva, lived for many years. (Information on who married whom is from John and Marguerite Black's book, *Ruch and the Upper Applegate Valley*.)

The photo of the Saltmarsh log house is one of my favorites. The workmanship with those logs is unbelievable. It is so sad that it was lost to fire in 1929. Of interest is Jason Hartman, who built the house in 1891 or 1892 and the barn in 1895, this being the same Jason Hartman who built the McKee Bridge in 1917.

[Editors' note: Sutherland was the husband of Victoria Florida Dunlap, cousin of Evelyn's great-grandfather, John McKee. John sued Sutherland to collect a debt and was the sole bidder at the sheriff's auction to satisfy the judgment. He got Sutherland's homestead for $400, and the extended McKee family moved there. Evelyn's mother, Pearl, was born on this land in 1894. John McKee died in the Eagle Hotel in 1911.]

The Eagle Hotel was a lively place built by Maude Pool's grandfather, Arthur Bird Pool. Evelyn copied this tintype from the collecion of Vieva Saltmash, wife of Arthur's grandson Glenn, in 1983.

Artheusa Evans Stafford, Arthur's second wife (far left), and Arthur Pool (middle) stand before the Eagle Hotel. Artheusa's daughter Alpha McDowell married Jason Hartman

Saltmarsh barn, 1895. Jaston Hartman is on the peak of the roof.
His cousin Benton Pool is second from the right.

Saltmarsh log house.

Remembering an Old Log Cabin

One of the best recent changes in my surroundings here on Palmer Creek Road is the elimination of the obnoxious star thistle weed on the Forest Service acreage adjacent to the north side of my property. Much credit is due to our local Forest Service botanist, Barbara Mumblo, who has had groups pulling the nasty weed for several years now. As I often take a walk by this area, the results give me much pleasure and bring back such fond memories.

These memories are of the old log cabin that sat on this piece of land, with its picturesque setting against the hillside. My mother told about her parents moving into it in 1889, with her two older brothers and her when she was four years old. The cabin was a three-room affair, with two small bedrooms. The bedrooms were portable, so to speak. The walls could be removed when the family wanted to have a neighborhood dance, a common entertainment in those days. The division walls and the floors were very interesting because they were of planed pine lumber 1¼ inches thick and 22½ inches wide.

Spring water was available from the mountain gulch behind the cabin. That saved digging a well for water as many pioneers had to do. There was a rock fireplace, but my mother didn't say if it was used for any cooking. It is hard to imagine a family of five living in such small quarters, especially during the winter, when they were more or less kept inside, as snow often reached the windowsills.

I don't know why or when they moved from there into another cabin about half a mile up the road near Palmer Creek, and then shortly after that to the Ray Mine near the headwaters of Palmer Creek. At this mine, they moved into a nice two-story log house, where my mother's sister Clara was born.

My grandfather was mining in Palmer Creek when he succeeded in finding a large gold nugget. With this nugget and a loan from Zack Cameron, he bought a 160-acre farm at the mouth of Palmer Creek in 1908. My home now sits on a small piece of the original property.

There is no way to know how many different people lived in that first log cabin. I do know that Valores and Helen Haskins were there for several years in the mid-1930s, and then Hiram Head lived there until the early 1950s. He was a wonderful neighbor, who liked to be of help, such as building a laundry bench for my mother to place her laundry tubs in. Years later, he built new kitchen cabinets for her but refused payment for his labor. Mother made sure he ate many meals with us through the years.

One time, when Mother needed to go to Medford, our car wouldn't start, so she contacted Hiram, and he offered to take Mother and me in his Whippet. It was quite old and only had one seat in front (the driver's seat), so mother and I had to sit on the floorboard in the back. I was somewhat embarrassed to be seen in such a vehicle. Nowadays that old car would be neat to ride in, say in a parade.

We never knew much about Hiram's background. My parents were careful about asking questions about one's personal life. It was not very neighborly to do so. We did know he had a daughter in Portland, who came to visit him one time, and when his health began to be a problem, he moved up there and we never heard of him again. That was sad; he had been such a good neighbor and loved living in that old cabin.*

Before he left, he wanted my dad to have his mining claim. My dad was not a miner but decided to do the assessment work in order to keep the property for a few years. When the Forest Service was tearing down old, unsafe buildings on mining claims here in the Applegate, my parents put a torch to the cabin. My mother saved a board from the cabin, which I now have, as a memento of her family once living there…back in time.

[*Editors' note: Hiram was born on Prince Edward Island, Canada, around 1870. He lived in Portland before coming to the Applegate in the late 1930s and died in Portland in 1955.]

Hiram Head in front of the cabin.

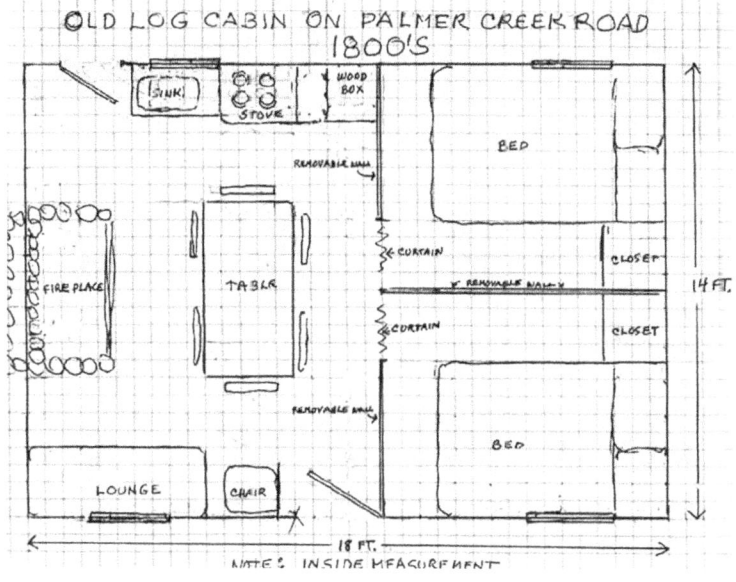

Floor plan drawn by Evelyn Byrne Williams.

My Great-granduncle Si McKee

Everybody has relatives who highlight most of their genealogical history in some way, with pride or sometimes with prejudice. There is one in my family who could be both—Silas Simon (Si) McKee. Born in Sullivan County, Missouri, in 1844 to Joseph and Almira McKee, nearly the youngest of eight children, he would hardly know his oldest brother, John M. McKee (my great-grandfather), born in 1827.

John M. and other relatives came west by wagon train, arriving in the Rogue Valley in 1853. Sometime in the mid 1860s John returned to Missouri to bring his parents and siblings west to Oregon. Along the way they met a family with a couple of wagons going to eastern Oregon, where they would need help floating down the Columbia River by barge to their final destination, the Willamette Valley. John's wagon train would be taking the Applegate Trail, which came farther south and avoided the Columbia River crossing. Parting ways with his family, Si, near the age of 20, hired on to help the other family complete their journey, knowing there was a possibility he would never see his family again.

He must have done all right because a few years later he turned up in the Illinois Valley driving a stage from Crescent City, California, to Grants Pass, Oregon. Sometimes when Uncle Si was in Grants Pass after a stage run, he would come by to visit his McKee relatives. My mother remembered him quite well and said everyone was so glad to see him. They never knew when he would show up on his horse, Nervy. He always seemed to be wearing a red kerchief around his neck, and he always had time to enjoy a game of checkers, cribbage, or pedro with the kids. When he sometimes took a nap on the couch, the kids said he snored louder than anyone they had ever heard. They would shake him awake, and he would tell them he was not asleep and had only closed his eyes to rest, making the kids laugh.

When the Gasquet Toll Road was completed in 1887, the Rockland Stage Stop (on the north side of the Smith River) and other stage stops went out of business, so Si lost his job. However, he was able to live in a cabin at the abandoned Rockland stop where he purchased some mining claims to mine for gold. That place soon became something of a permanent residence where he was able to exist quite well with salmon in the North Fork of the Smith River and some trout in other streams. Also deer and bear, along with pigeon and grouse, gave him all the protein he needed. Some edible plants and berries along with beans (I am sure) filled out his menu nicely.

Si had fallen in love with the area and refused to move closer to his many relatives in the Rogue Valley. He never married, but the family believed there was a girl, named Kathleen, sometime in his past, because when he was visiting relatives one time, they played a phonograph record of "I'll take you home again, Kathleen," and he broke down crying. He would not tell them why.

Eventually he moved away from Rockland, probably because it had been sold, and he went to Sourdough where he continued his mining occupation at Diamond Creek and Bald Face Creek, all still in the Smith River drainage. This large area is mostly government land where cattlemen free-ranged their cattle. Heavy forest is not good forage, but open space created by fire is. Thus Si's life was about to change.

For several years increasing fires in this area began to worry the government and an investigation was launched. It was decided that Si was hired by the cattlemen to start fires to make more grazing spaces, a common practice in those days. Si was arrested for arson and sent to jail. He never revealed his association with the cattlemen to the authorities. While in jail, his relatives laughed about him being able to have a better bed, meals, reading material, and a good long rest.

He eventually returned to his mining operations, and the forest recovered from the fires. The authorities and the relatives were relieved that Si had reformed. Unfortunately, Si does not ride pleasantly off into the sunset.

To be continued…

Great-granduncle Si, stage driver turned miner, among other things.

Uncle Si lived in this cabin at the abandoned Rockland Stage Stop, where he mined for gold.

The Last of Great-granduncle Si

In mid-October 1922, Si visited some relatives living on 25 acres of very productive bottomland near Bear Creek at Tolo, where Fort Lane was located during the Rogue River War. He now owned a small horse named Nellie and an Australian shepherd named Jiggs. However, when he came out of the mountains to visit, he would leave Nellie at Waldo and then ride the "jitney" on into Medford, where presumably he walked to Tolo. The relatives always enjoyed Si's visits but were a little concerned about his habit of carrying gold nuggets on his person.

Not only did he have the gold nuggets, but also he talked about his nuggets and gold dust that he kept in a tin can at his cabin. They advised him to deposit his cache in a safe place, but he didn't "cotton" to banks, and, besides, he kept his small pistol close at hand. Many of the old-timers never really trusted banks and often buried their gold somewhere in a hidden place near their dwellings. Si did, however, leave a handwritten note giving his mining claim to the family living there at Tolo.

One time when Uncle Si came to visit, he had a young man with him that he had met in Waldo. The family was concerned when he said that the young man was going to go home with him to help do some mining. And they were right to be worried about Si—in the third week of November they were notified by the authorities that he had been killed (shot?) in his cabin. Some friends had become suspicious when they had not seen him for quite some time and contacted the local police. When police arrived at the cabin, they found his emaciated dog, Jiggs, guarding the cabin. In order to go in, they had to shoot him. They also shot the horse, which hadn't had food for so long he was not savable.

They buried the remains of Uncle Si, 78, near his cabin and advised the relatives to visit the cabin site and take care of necessities. I was told that my grandfather, Amos McKee, and his son, Ernest, rode horseback from there on the Upper Applegate to Sourdough. The young man whom Si had taken with him from Waldo was never found, and the general opinion was that he killed Si for those nuggets and maybe the can of gold dust, which was never found, either.

After Si's death a kind man working on the road near the grave felt badly that no one had made a marker, so he found Si's old metal bed frame and made a crude fence around the grave from its parts. Then as more time went by, another kind soul wanted to give Si a marker with his name on it. The metal marker says McGee instead of McKee, but the relatives appreciated it regardless of the wrong name. Years later my husband, Clarence, and I visited the mining claim and the remains of the cabin. The road was so bad that we needed four-wheel-drive, and in some places I got out of the vehicle and walked rather than being bounced all over. As I stood looking at the grave site, my mind raced back to when Great-granduncle Si had contentedly lived there so many years, and I was sad for his tragic death. I was also saddened by the fact that his marker was gone and only some of the bent and rusty supports of the old fence were there.

While doing research on Uncle Si and his Sourdough claim, I went to the Del Norte Museum in Crescent City. I was looking for old photos of the early-day stagecoaches and drivers. I didn't find any of Uncle Si, but much to my delight, I saw the old grave "McGee" marker in one of the glass cases.

*Roland Hubbard crossing the Smith River
in Uncle Si's hand-hewn canoe, August 1913.*

A crossing on the Smith River near Uncle Si's cabin.

Farming in the Forties, Part One

Quite a few years back I copied a diary that Cary Culy had written in 1946 and 1947. It isn't that old, but it certainly shows the lifestyle of early farmers here in the Applegate. Cary came into this world at Hayfork, California. The family moved north to Steamboat, in a remote area of the Applegate, where his father, George, and mother, Permelia, had a 120-acre homestead on which to build a house and barns in about 1882. They also had the Steamboat Post Office and boarded the schoolteachers who taught the Culys' six children and others at the Steamboat School.

In 1905 Cary married Verna McKee, daughter of Deb and Leila McKee, for whom the historic McKee Bridge is named. In 1910 Cary and Verna bought the 50-acre farmland on Kinney Creek, across the river from Mule Mountain. It was not the loamy, fertile ground that every farmer wishes for, and much work was needed to improve the land in order to make a living from it. There were always wagon loads of unwanted rocks to haul away after plowing and loads of manure to be spread over the ground for successful crops each year. Water for irrigation traveled down a long ditch from the river to the fields. The ditch was always in need of cleaning or patching or the water in need of being switched from field to field.

Cary and Verna were neighbors of my family, both living on the west side of the Applegate River, only a couple of miles apart. However, getting to their farm was not easy. The road on the west side ended near our house, so they had to use the main road on the east side of the river and then cross a footbridge. The bridge was about 1/8 mile from their house. Everything had to be brought across the bridge: farm equipment, home items, groceries.

The Culys had four children: Omar, Helen, Louis, and Leora. Omar, the oldest, was the only one who stayed and worked on the farm until marrying much later in life. He was a tremendous worker for his parents, as witnessed in Cary's diary. Of the daily entries, I have chosen just a few I found of interest. Here is a glimpse into the Culys' life on Kinney Creek.

Tues. Jan 1, 1946—Weather clear

Omar and I hung the shoulders and side meat this morning and cleaned the trash out of the smoke house and put the heater stove in for to build the fire in to smoke the meat got done about 11:30 am. We didn't do anything only I put the license on the car and brought the double trees over from Edd's. [Ed Finley, a good friend and neighbor, lived across the river near the footbridge.] Omar caught a muskrat.

Wed. Jan 2, 1946—Rain

Omar and I got the lumber from the loft over the horses to make bottom for the wagon box and after dinner Omar and I went up and got the sides of the sluice box that was up at first gulch and we loosened the bolts in the wagon box. Omar went to his traps and set 1 more trap.

Mon. Jan 7, 1946—Rain

Omar and I did the chores and I trimmed the horses tails and we hauled a load of oak wood am and Omar and I raised the broke ratchet on the wagon pm and fixed the little chicken house that Lewis built so the little calve could go in it pm It rained the most of the time today and snowed a little this evening.

124

Sat. Jan 12, 1946—Clear

Omar and I hauled five loads of manure. Omar got some smoke wood while I was unloading 1 load. We are going to grange this evening. We got home 2 am Sunday.

Mon. Jan 28, 1946—Cloudy

The ground was white with snow and about 1 inch in J'ville I took Uncle Stephen over to Medford. Omar helped Edd saw wood. I got 4 sacks of seed oats and sack barley a pruning saw and long handle pruner.

Tues. Jan 29, 1946—Cloudy, snow, showers

Omar helped Edd cut wood. I cleaned out south end of the big barn. Lee Port [Forest Service Ranger at Star Ranger Station] come up and marked the trees that [he] wanted for wood. I drove over to the foot bridge at 3:30 pm. Omar packed the seed oats over and a sack of barley.

Sat. Feb 23, 1946—Clear

I hauled 3 loads of manure Omar picked pruning sprouts and Omar and I got a load of gravel and put it on each side of the bridge over by Kinney Creek gate. We went to the dance [at Upper Applegate Grange Hall, near McKee Bridge] in evening.

Tues. April 30, 1946—Clear

Viola [Ed's wife], Omar, Verna and I went to Medford. We took the washing machine engine over to the May Tag for a over haul it cost $11.10 for the over haul and a gal of oil. I bought a riding bridle and bit $3.75. I let Omar have $10.00.

[Then there were these most interesting entries]

Wed. June 19, 1946—Clear

I mowed and raked hay. Omar and Edd shocked some on the piece above the telephone line. I took Verna to see if we could see Dr. Bishop. Helen [their daughter] got Bishop on the line about 11 pm and we got home about 1 am Thursday.

Fri. June 21, 1946—Clear

I mowed and raked hay Omar and Edd mowed with the scythe and shocked hay. Rosley [daughter-in-law] took Verna over to the Dr. and Verna went to the hospital.

Tues. June 25, 1946—Mostly cloudy

I finished mowing about 11 am. Edd and Omar turned winnows and some with scythe and shocked a little a.m. and pm I raked hay and shocked all afternoon. Rosley went over to the hospital after Verna and then brought 900 square ft of insaneating [?] plank 2 sacks of cement and roll of asphalt siding back on trailer.

And that is all we will ever know about Verna's illness, but the story continues in the next "Back in Time." There is a shooting, and electricity comes to the Upper Applegate.

Cary and Verna (McKee) Culy, sometime in the 1940s.

Farming in the Forties, Part Two

We left off with Verna Culy coming home after a few days in the hospital. And just like last time we are still in the dark as to why she needed to go. Cary Culy's diary continues with the more important business of ranching, and a very busy Verna.

Oct 1, 1946—temp a.m. 46°—cloudy

Omar and I hauled 38 posts from up on the hill above Witters place. Verna canned meat 19 qts. And cooked some berries for jelly. It rained a good shower last night enough to settle the dust. Edd went upon the hill this morning. Verna hung some meat to dry.

Nov 14, 1946—clear

Verna, Omar, Viola and I went to Medford. We paid our taxes $44.52. Verna let Omar have $10.00 I bought a bottle for $3.00.

Dec 21, 1946—temp 28°

Omar and I did chores and worked 2 hrs. on the road down on the big turn across from Morris Byrne's a.m. and we worked about 2 hours on the road this after noon.

[At this time the Culys were still building, by hand, a road to connect them to the end of Palmer Creek Road. Once this was done, they no longer needed to transport everything across the river on a swinging bridge and walk a quarter mile to the house.]

Dec 25, 1946—temp 35°

Omar, Verna and I went over to Edd's and Leora's [son-in-law and daughter] for dinner those that was there Ernie, Helen [son-in-law and daughter], Roney, Russell [grandsons], Lewis. Rosley [son and daughter-in-law], Mary, Charles [grandchildren], and Orval White and family and Bob Rooker. Ernie and Helen got me a wool jacket, Roney and Russell got me a pipe I got a box of candy from Lewis and Rosely and Edd and Leora got me a 12 in. cresent rinch. Bob Rooker got me 2 pair of socks. Omar got me a tie and a diary book.

Jan 3, 1947—temp 16

Omar and I boarded up around under the sills of the house and I pulled the hay out of the way where we are feeding out of. Omar put a shelf up in his bedroom a.m. P.m. Omar, Charles and I worked on the road. I put in about 1 hr. Charles and Omar worked 2 hrs and 45 min. Daily and his father and 2 women came to look at the place. [The Culys were thinking about selling and moving to Jacksonville.]

Jan 29, 1947—temp 32°

Omar helped feed and went up Kinney Creek Divide. He rode Twister up to the top and turned him loose and he come home. Omar went down Strait Gulch to where we killed the cougar and up to Chimey Gulch gap and around and down Canacker [now Kanaka Gulch]. I finished the chores and worked 2 ½ hrs. on the road a.m. P.m. I went over and got the mail

March 9, 1947—temp 43°—rain

Started raining about 5 and has been raining steady until 7:30 and is still raining hard. Omar and I started the cattle up in the oaks this morning got back 11 a.m. And finished the chores and that about all we done except chores. Omar went over to Scovills this after noon. [Mr. Scovill worked for the local power company, COPCO.] After Grange we danced until about 1:30 a.m. there was some folks come from Ruch 2 from Eagle Point and one from Ruch. They played acorden, a electric steel guytar and a drum. There were 54 there for lunch. Verna, Omar, Fred Dorn and I was on the serving comitty.

Apr 27, 1947—temp 37°—clear a.m./cloudy p.m.

Rained a good shower this evening. Omar and I drove the milk cow up to where Harthen has his tent and we hauled manure and cleaned the weeds and rocks off the corn ground and we butchered Hats calf this evening. Hard's [Lyle Hard's] little boy [Billy?] got his hand blew off with a giant powder cap. [The Hard family lived near McKee Bridge behind the store.] The telephone out fit went on strike in Medford.

May 28, 1947—cloudy

I irrigated and mowed hay for the stock and pulled the runners of the strawberries. Omar, Verna and I went to the grange hall to a meeting for electricy the Copco man was there and gave us the figures on what it would cost us.

June 22, 1947—temp 46°—clear

36 loads of alfaly first crop. Omar, Edd, Charles and I hauled 3 loads of hay this morning. Lewis and Polky helped with 2 loads. Polky and Lucile [Lewis's daughter] come about 9 a.m. I went up to first gulch and turned what water there was down but that wasn't much. I put it on the pasture. Leora, Soney, and Eddie come out 9:30 a.m. Albert Culy come about 12 noon and went back 3 p.m. and the rest of them left shortly after Albert did and Omar, Verna and I went up and cleaned the rack and there wasn't much water and we went on up to the waist gate at Jolly's and found the pipe across from Bert Harr's was blocked and it took us about 2 hrs to clean it out. We got home about 7 p.m. and I fixed to run the water by the foot bridge.

July 24, 1947—temp 44°—clear/cloudy

I put the kind shoes on twister this morning and mowed sweet clover the rest of the four noon and I mowed sweet clover p.m. Omar cut 2 poles for the electric line and 3 poles and done some weeding.

[From this time on Omar has cut about a dozen poles for the future electricity. Each family wanting electricity had to furnish so many poles and dig the holes for them. By October 23 the Culys were getting fixtures for the future electricity and on November 16 they were installing a hot water heater.]

Aug 20, 1947

I irrigated and I took Omar up to help Albert Collings with his hay and I took Charles home. We left for Medford about 9 a.m. and I got back home 11:45. I brought back 75# of ice and 3 sacks of barley, 2 sacks for Omar. Martin Pierce shot him self accidentally and died instantly. [Unfortunately, I have no other information about Martin. He may have lived near Forest Creek on Hwy 238, where a family by the name of Pierce lived.]

The last part of Cary's diary had many pages of the names of people working on cutting poles, slashing, digging holes, and measuring for wire. Electricity was finally coming to the Culy farm and to all of their neighbors in 1947.

Thanks to Russell and Melba McIntyre for the loan of this diary

The picture of the Upper Applegate Grange Hall, located next to McKee Bridge, shows where the Culys and many Applegaters came for community events like dancing and for information about local or national issues important to their area. Picture taken November 17, 1940.

Upper Grange Hall, 1940
Back row, L-R: Bert Harr, John Norris, Frank Bowman,
Lee C. Port, Louis Culy, Morris Byrne, Hiram Head, Dow Lewis.
Middle row, L-R: Cary Culy, Verna (McKee) Culy, Osie Cantrall, Grace Buck, Thelma Young,
Clara (McKee) Smith, Albert Collings, Alma Collings, Metta Buck, Valoris Haskins, Helen Haskins,
Amos McKee, Charlotte "Lottie" (Pence) McKee, Florence Byrne, Slim Perry, Bertha Haskins,
Evelyn Byrne, Clara Faye McKee, Helen Thomas, Ellouise Nomer.
Front row, L-R: Gladys Byrne, Pearl (McKee) Byrne, Maud Port, Fred Dorn, Albert Young,
James Winningham, Edward Finley ("Edd" in Cary's diary), Floyd McKee, Wallace Haskins,
John Byrne, Harry Mallott, Christine (Beaver) Harr, Mamie (Watkins) Winningham, Omar Culy,
Eva McKee, Rosalie Culy "(Rosley" in Cary's diary).

Cure-alls at Cinnabar Springs

This magical place, Cinnabar Springs, where the "healthy water" was drunk and bathed in to take care of all kinds of illnesses back in the old days, was located in the Siskiyou Mountains just south of the Oregon-California border. Some interesting old photos show people staying there for long periods of time in temporary quarters they made from supplies brought with them. My Byrne family was there several times in the early 1900s. They went on horseback over the mountains from their home on Squaw Creek. How I wish I had asked them more about that time in their life. Evidently drinking the Cinnabar water didn't do them any harm, but did it do them any good? It contained the principal ore of mercury, a mineral and mercuric sulfide.

In one of my scrapbooks I found this account written by Drew Clerin for the *Medford Mail Tribune* about 1958. I find it too interesting to leave any of it out, so here it is.

"During the summer of 1907, our family—father, mother and five kids— camped out at Cinnabar Springs. We took with us from Portland two tents, sundry camping equipment, and supplies of all sorts sufficient for our two-month stay. I remember that we purchased canvas, cut it up into bed sizes and installed grommets through which rope would run to fasten the canvas mattresses to frames which we planned to construct from small logs at our destination. They worked like a charm.

"My dad cashed a check at the bank and brought home a stack of $20 gold pieces, ten in number, which was sufficient to pay for transportation and living expenses for our two-month camping trip.

"We took the Southern Pacific train to Medford, then the narrow gauge from Medford to Jacksonville, and a horse-drawn vehicle from Jacksonville to the Saltmarsh farm on the Applegate River. We five youngsters slept in the hay in the Saltmarsh barn. Early next morning, Mr. Saltmarsh saddled the horses, loaded the pack animals, and we headed south over some 20 miles or so of narrow mountain trails, across the California line a couple of miles to Cinnabar Springs.

"The horses and mules knew every inch of the trail and never so much as stumbled on the rocky trail over the Siskiyou divide between the Applegate and Klamath River watersheds.

"Cinnabar Springs was located in a rugged canyon through which ran a beautiful mountain stream, one of the forks of Beaver Creek that flows into the Klamath. The entire area was covered with the most beautiful stand of sugar pine I have ever seen. I was only twelve, and seven of these years were spent in Aberdeen, Washington, at the turn of the century. Aberdeen in 1900 was in the heart of the Douglas fir forest of the Olympic peninsula, and stands of virgin timber were beautiful to behold, but the sugar pine in the Cinnabar area was majestic beyond description and made an impression on me that will last my lifetime.

"The main mineral spring was roofed over by an octagon-shaped spring house, open at the sides, with benches that surrounded the pool, which was five or six feet in diameter. Each of the men who was taking the mineral water cure had staked out squatter's rights to a seat on the bench. Each had an empty quart size tomato can to serve as a drinking cup, and behind his seat he tacked a piece of paper on which he tallied the number of quarts consumed each day. The can was dipped in the pool, the contents consumed, and a tally mark entered on the sheet.

"Par for the course, as I remember, was in the neighborhood of twenty quarts a day. Competition was fierce in the matter of establishing and beating records for liquid consumption. These old gentlemen spent hours on the spring house bench. Numerous and varied were the topics discussed, and a great deal of boasting was indulged in on the subject of their liquid capacity.

"One old fellow was the acknowledged champion of the entire field with a specialty no one could equal. He would fill his quart can to the brim and down the entire contents without removing it from his lips. With highly charged, ice-cold mineral water, this was an accomplishment which was the envy of all the other contestants. Of course, he would only perform if a suitable audience were present.

"Generally, there were ten to twelve couples who participated in the Saturday night dances. Square dances were the rule, and often one or two youngsters were recruited to fill out the squares. It was my impression that the quicksilver mine on the ridge at the south was practically a one-man operation. Gossip had it that the mine owner shipped out his flasks of quicksilver in the early fall, one on each side of a mule packsaddle. The pack train was driven over the Siskiyou summit to Jacksonville, six or so mules making up the train. On the return trip, each mule was supposed to have carried two kegs of whiskey, which was the winter supply for the mine owner. I know that several of the ladies at the camp were shocked at the amount of whiskey required for one winter's use. They were quite sure that the mine owner—I have forgotten his name—would drink himself to death. Perhaps he did. He was in his 80s at the time. I have neglected a comment on the qualities of the healthy water. I cannot vouch personally for the medicinal virtues of Cinnabar Springs mineral water, but I can talk with authority about its quality.

"The water in the main spring was ice cold and so highly charged with soda that it would bubble through one's nose like champagne. After drinking it for several days one would develop a taste for it to the extent that ordinary pure-mountain water suffered by comparison.

"I remember that after we returned to Portland on some of the hot September days, I would develop a craving for Cinnabar Springs water that Bull Run could not satisfy.

"Cinnabar Springs is still within the borders of the Klamath National Forest, and it is possible that so-called progress has not yet polluted the beautiful streams and destroyed the sugar pine forest."

I also wonder what it looks like today. It was over fifty years ago that my husband and I went there one day hoping to find what was left. I don't remember there being much. I was more interested in the drive getting there. Too bad that I did not take any photos of at least what remains.

Bill Anderson second from left, Maud Kubli with the white cup, and
Eleanor Turvey with Edward and Edith Kubli on the right.

John, Stella, and Katie Byrne camping at Cinnabar Springs in 1908
with Bruce Buck, Patrick J. Sullivan, and other unidentified friends.

Among these seventy-seven campers taking the cure
at Cinnabar Springs are Byrnes, Buckleys, Bruce Buck, and P.J. Sullivan.

About the Editors

Applegater Newsmagazine

Diana Coogle is chair of the *Applegater* newsmagazine, which was founded in 1994 as part of the Northwest Forest Plan. The *Applegater*, officially the Applegate Valley Community Newsmagazine, later became a 501(c)(3) organization on its own.

The paper, delivered free, on a quarterly basis, to all residents and businesses in the Applegate, has long been cherished by its readers. By editorial policy, all articles must be relevant specifically to the Applegate. In keeping with its mission to enhance the quality of life in the Applegate "through honest, constructive, relevant, and entertaining reports on a wide variety of subjects and viewpoints, including our natural resources, historical and current events, and community news," the *Applegater* is pleased to add *Back in Time* to the other book we have published, *From the Heart of the Applegate*, an anthology of prose and poetry from Applegate writers. Visit us and read past and current issues at applegater.org.

McKee Bridge Historical Society

Laura Ahearn is president of the McKee Bridge Historical Society (MBHS), an idea born at a dinner party in the home of Evelyn Byrne Williams and her husband, Clarence, on January 7, 1999. Although McKee Bridge is owned by Jackson County, local Applegate residents and nongovernmental organizations had long assumed responsibility for maintaining the historic structure. For example, in 1965, the Upper Applegate Grange and Knights of Pythias supplied funds and volunteer labor for a new roof.

In 1985 Jackson County announced it would no longer provide funding to preserve the bridge. Local residents who cherished the bridge did not give up. Forty-two citizens met at the Star Ranger Station on October 26, 1987, to form the Save McKee Bridge Committee. The group launched many fundraisers, and Evelyn designed the McKee Bridge Quilt (crafted with her mother, 92-year-old Pearl McKee Byrne, and neighbor Bonnie Connelly) to recognize major donors.

MBHS continues to provide the maintenance and inspections required to keep McKee Bridge open and preserves and shares relics and stories from the entire Applegate watershed. Visit mckeebridge.org and tour the Virtual Museum to learn more.

Index of Photographs